SIMCOX, Kenneth
A town at war: Shrewsbury, 1939-45

A TOWN AT WAR

Shrewsbury 1939 – 1945

by

Kenneth Simcox

Shropshire Libraries

1983

The author wishes to acknowledge the help received in preparing this booklet from Mrs. A. Hay and the late Mr. E. Hay, Mrs. Eileen Davies, Mr. Alan Morgan, and the staff of the Local Studies Library, Shrewsbury. The publishers would like to thank the County Archivist for permission to reproduce newspaper advertisements and extracts from wartime propaganda from the collection of Mrs. Mary Chitty. The two Council Minutes are from the Local Studies Library, Shropshire Libraries.

ISBN 0 903802 25 2
Cover design: Joyce Fogg
Published by Shropshire Libraries,
London Road, Shrewsbury.
Printed at The Shirehall, Shrewsbury.
© Kenneth Simcox 1983

Simcox, Kenneth
A town at war: Shrewsbury, 1939–45
1. Shrewsbury — History
I. Title
942.4'54   DA690.S58

ISBN 0-903802-25-2

CONTENTS

"...
For we're fed up with your trickery
And we'll dig like smoke for victory.
We're after you, Herr Adolf, with a spade".

Concluding lines of the Marching Song for Victory,
composed after a 'Dig for Victory' meeting in
Shrewsbury Castle, 8th February 1941.

Introduction: 1939–1945

A different age from ours, in Shrewsbury as elsewhere.

For instance, take a look inside the shops. The chemists (privately owned most of them) with their dark shelves. Bile beans to keep us fresh, youthful and vital. Vibronita, Nature's Restorative, Iron-Ox, Parkinson's Pills, Solidox toothpaste. Puritan soap purchasable for a twelve-sided threepenny bit and a tiny farthing. Then Beetox Extract next door at the grocer's (7d and 1/4d) and Mazawattee tea.

Cigarettes on sale without government health warnings; indeed without warnings from any of the quarters from which they emanate in the 1980s. Horse racing at Bayston Hill, and Midland League football beside the River Severn. An age when 'Yes my darling daughter' could be billed as the sauciest comedy seen on the screen, when the Marx Brothers were widely considered second-rate, and when a film could be given the title 'The Gay Sisters' without causing the raising of a single eyebrow.

In 1939 a housewife could price the furniture in Shrewsbury (dining chair 10/6, table 43/6, dining suite £7.7.0., bedroom suite £8.17.6. at Astons), then compare prices elsewhere by laying out 1/7d on a return railway ticket to Wolverhampton. An extra 3d would have carried her to Birmingham and back. Then, as now, coach excursions were extremely popular. On that fateful Sunday morning of 3rd September 1939, Midland Red were running trips to Dudley Zoo and Dolgelly, and times have not changed in that respect; however, a run to Dorrington and Pulverbatch, even if we disregard the 1/- fare, is hardly an outing that would take place in the 1980s. In that September of 1939 a mere £5.18.6. would have given the holiday-maker a week in Weston-super-Mare by courtesy of Salopia Tours; but at £225 for an Austin Twelve, new cars were relatively expensive.

Attend to the 'sits. vac.' in the local newspapers, or at Mary Neale's registry in Claremont Street, or Reads' agency on Wyle Cop. A senior typist with the Salop County Council might command £110 per annum, a maidservant in Kennedy Road £48-£65. As late as 1944 a cook-housekeeper could look forward to no more than £78, while the following year a 56-year old domestic, in receipt of the same wages for the past thirty-five years – namely £1 per week less insurance – with one afternoon a week off and alternate Sundays, was heard to enquire whether such was the best Shrewsbury could offer. "If only I had a home" she added (poignantly). But it was not only the wages. Nothing illustrates the dubious status enjoyed by the working classes better than the ads. of the period. In demand were "strong handy" men and "strong willing" girls, "smart" boys and "clean refined" girls. "Good general wanted" advertised a certain well-heeled employer in September 1939, which was truer than he (or indeed anyone else, except possibly Winston Churchill) suspected.

Nowadays we have grown accustomed to the statutory protection which is our children's right. Not so then when a baby could be put on the market in the same way as an electric cooker or a second-hand car. "Healthy baby girl, one month, for adoption", "good home wanted for baby girl, five months", "middle-aged couple good home will adopt baby". So the adverts. ran. It seems as if not only the young but the old were sometimes more readily accorded charity than the dignity of human rights; the Mayor's Christmas 1943 Fund enabled 1,340 old people and children to be entertained at the Granada Cinema and to receive 1/- each to take home with them.

Insensitivity to the dignity of others also marked the everyday use of words nowadays regarded as offensive. Oswestry Orthopaedic could quite unashamedly be referred to as the Cripples' Hospital, while 'nigger' and 'darkie' were quite commonplace epithets. But contempt for far-flung foreign breeds was generally widespread. 1939–45 was the first period in history when Britishers in vast numbers descended on territories often far beyond the confines of Europe. The world was a larger place forty years ago, and living conditions among the millions of poor in Cairo, Baghdad and Bombay took the troops by surprise. What it did not do, as the writer can testify, was call forth sympathy for our newly-found brothers. Scorn for the 'wog' was traditional among the occupying armies who apostrophised him as a despicable object entirely responsible for his own degradation.

We have grown wiser than that since then – perhaps. On the other hand, perhaps not, for who can see the present in perspective? The historian has the advantage over the commentator in that the former is in a position to deride the judgements of the past. In March 1940 the French were boasting of the special, uncrackable cement used in the construction of the Maginot Line: "this was still a secret from the Germans". The following two months are rich in such examples. "In France", announced the Shrewsbury Chronicle of 29th March, "there has been a change of government which implies no weakening. M. Paul Reynaud, the new prime minister, is hailed as a man of action who will leave no stone unturned to obtain a speedy victory". And a fortnight later, with regard to the German invasion of Denmark and Norway: "The allies have lost no time in dealing with the situation".

If we are to benefit from our interpretation of history, self-satisfaction needs to be tempered with humility.

"They did not knock the Cliffs of Dover"

"Within twenty-four hours the life of the town was changed by mobilisation. Uniforms everywhere, shops busier, increased spending power, every day a market day . . ." and "Gone is the carnival and the holiday spirit but there is a finer enthusiasm and a greater joy – that of service. There are no glum faces, no nervousness, no depression". Thus the Shrewsbury Chronicle of 15th September 1939, taking stock a fortnight after Hitler's invasion of Poland. A great adventure (such was the implication) was afoot; and indeed the ironic truth is that after a long period of declining morale Britain had been given a life-enhancing injection. As if to redeem future mortalities, soon there was an epidemic of marriages, and the birth-rate began to soar. As if to emphasise Shrewsbury's regained vitality, newcomers also helped swell the population. And as if to proclaim a new, more extrovert approach to life, admissions to Shelton (the local psychiatric hospital) took a sharp downward turn.

Here was an example of a change being better than a rest; and change was what marked local as well as national and international affairs at this time – to which the streets of Shrewsbury bore witness. The earliest of these strange sights was of civilians (itself a new concept) carrying their gas-masks: in cardboard containers at first although these, in the case of fashion-conscious young women, were soon to be replaced by more exotic designs. An ephemeral change, however. Within a month the habit of carrying gas-masks had been successfully kicked, and few were seen thereafter.

As the war progressed, more and more khaki and blue uniforms were seen in the streets, and from 1942 the smoother cloth of the American servicemen became commonplace. But perhaps the most revolutionary change of all and the one most difficult to become accustomed to was the sight of women in their new roles. Servicewomen of course, and Women's Land Army, ATS redcaps; women not in skirts but trousers doing 'men's' jobs, for example women telephone engineers and women street sweepers in their khaki smocks and slacks. There were fifty postwomen in Shrewsbury by 1942, and October of that year saw (or heard) the first female announcer at the railway station. The town's first policewoman was recruited in May 1944 – rather later than in some places; back in February 1943 a cartoon had shown a policewoman apprehending an offender with the words "Now will you come quietly or shall I scream?". Women in general must have found it infuriating. But then, male chauvinism has seldom been slow to manifest itself in any age. 'The Guvnor' writing in the Chronicle on 11th February 1944 had observed ATS girls on a morning run in their shorts. He commented "As I have remarked before, this is a remarkable kind of war".

On 6th November 1940 King George VI and Queen Elizabeth toured the bombed areas of Merseyside, and the Queen was observed to admire the view of the Severn downstream towards the Castle Bridge as the royal train passed slowly through Shrewsbury railway station. The King repeated the same journey on 17th December, but this time on his own. What the Princess Royal thought of Harlescott when she inspected ATS there on 31st March 1944 we do not know; she had visited the town previously in March 1940 and May 1941, and Lady Mountbatten had followed suit, but alas with those brief glimpses of royalty and its connections Shrewsbury had to rest content.

Strange today to think of cattle being driven through a town's main streets: a medieval practice surely? Yet with Shrewsbury's livestock market (the Smithfield) then near the town centre, cattle regularly ambled along Castle Street and down Dogpole and Wyle Cop. In April 1942 a cow wriggled free of its constraints, knocked over a woman in Mardol, and charged in the direction of the Quarry where it was discovered quietly browsing. Thus was wartime bustle punctuated by more bucolic moments. Horses and drays too were familiar sights, as was Jessie the beloved donkey from the Ditherington Maltings, who used to pull a little orange cart and whose ultimate act of war service was to give the children of Meole Brace rides at their VE Day party.

One effect of the war was that a great number of public buildings were put to new uses. Hardly had it begun than the Ministry of Supply (Aluminium Control) had installed one hundred and fifty civil servants in the town's principal hotel, the Raven, where they remained until 1943. For the remainder of the war the Raven functioned as an American services club. Fifty yards away the Crown was, for eighteen months from November 1940, in the hands of Pearl Assurance who also took over part of Attingham Hall. Another stone's throw distant, the Royal Salop Infirmary was prepared for use as a base hospital; as such it received early casualties from the Normandy landings in June 1944, together with Copthorne. The latter, which was put up as a temporary military hospital, survives today as part of the Royal Shrewsbury. In March 1944 Radbrook Hall, now a hotel, was converted into a rest home for sick factory workers.

With Shrewsbury School hosting five hundred scholars from Cheltenham College, the latter's red-tasselled mortar-boards became a feature of the area. The Music Hall filled up with office furniture as the Army Pay Corps moved in, the old Wyle Cop Schools were taken over as a recruiting centre, and a Citizens' Advice Bureau was set up in Princess Street. The opening of the new County Buildings in the Square on 3rd February 1940 would have taken place regardless of the war; not so the commandeering of the swimming baths the same year, a move which aroused anger on the part of parents fearful of the consequences of their children resorting to river swimming. The siting of the British Restaurant away from the town centre in Ditherington also came in for strong criticism, and when in May 1941 the remains of historic St. Austin Friars were demolished without warning it was the turn of the antiquarians and archaeologists to be up in arms.

Reverting to the changing function of buildings, no more radical change occurred than at the Ditherington Maltings, the world's first iron-framed construction and a one-time flax mill. With a brief interlude in 1932–33 malt had been produced there since 1898, then in 1939 it became an army training barracks for recruits, with a large war map displayed on an outside wall, a rock garden and flower beds: a prettier prospect at any rate than the scrap-metal dumps that adorned Barker Street, Argyll Street and Greyfriars Road. A point of attraction, always, was the most enterprising store in Shrewsbury – Maddox's. No soooner had the phoney war become unphoney than Maddox's did all they could for public morale with some fascinating displays including in August 1940 a Heinkel bomber shot down near Birmingham; thousands flocked to see it.

The year 1945 saw establishments which had been set up gradually being dismantled. Organisations such as the London office of the Canadian Pacific Railway which had been evacuated in 1940 (working from what was then Ridgebourne Hotel in Kennedy Road) returned to base. War-time units such as RAF Monkmoor closed down. As soon as all threat from enemy incendiaries had been eliminated, the Theatre Royal in Shoplatch decided to stage a devastating fire which burnt away the roof and left the whole of the balcony open to the sky. Again, shortly after VE Day, as if in astonishment that what had gone on so long was at last over, on his high column at the junction of Abbey Foregate and London Road, Lord Hill's arm fell off. The council decided to replace it with a safer, wooden one. "We have", announced the lady chairman of the Estates Committee, "taken the precaution of making sure than no other parts of the gentleman's anatomy will fall off". There was, a relieved public decided, no answer to that.

POTATO PLAN. PART 5

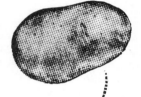

How to use potatoes in place of flour

when you bake a cake

Here's a flour-saving cake recipe, using grated raw potatoes in place of part of the flour. It makes a lovely spicy cake — be sure to try it!

FAMILY CAKE

3 oz. sugar, 3 oz. margarine, 3 oz. grated raw potato, pinch of salt, ½ teaspoon mixed spice, a little vanilla essence, 2 eggs (reconstituted), 6-oz. flour, 4 oz. chopped dates or sultanas, 1 teaspoon baking powder.

METHOD: Cream sugar and margarine, add potato, beat well. Add salt, spice and vanilla essence. Beat in the eggs, and flour, add fruit, and baking powder. Place in a greased tin, bake in a moderate oven for 1½ hours.

THE 4 OTHER PARTS OF THE PLAN

1 Serve potatoes for breakfast on three days a week.

2 Make your main dish a potato dish one day a week.

3 Refuse second helpings of other foods — have more potatoes instead.

4 Make a point of serving potatoes in other ways than "plain boiled."

Flour costs ships . . .
Use home-grown potatoes instead

ISSUED BY THE MINISTRY OF FOOD, LONDON, W.1
P.25

Before the beginning of the war Lord Hill's column, in common with many other edifices, was enclosed by railings; indeed we scarcely realise, in an age when they have to a great extent disappeared, the degree to which railings were once a feature of the townscape. Largely they disappeared because their metal was needed for armaments, but disappear without a fight they did not. From 1940 until 1943 the 'Railings Controversy' raged, with the churches at the centre of the argument. Why, asked 'The Guvnor' in the Shrewsbury Chronicle of 2nd August 1940, did churches need railings round them when pubs did not? A good question! Anticipating the compulsory order of October 1941 St. Mary's got rid of theirs six months previously and planted privet instead, but not all were as speedy. Ironically, after all the fuss, complaints were heard that some of the metal had gone to put up new gates at government department buildings!

The great food-growing campaign was on from the moment in September 1939 that the War Agricultural Committee appealed for as much land as possible to be ploughed, the only reservation in certain minds being the manner in which footpaths and rights of way were quietly being lost in the process. In Shrewsbury allotments proliferated – in Sundorne Road, Copthorne, Coton Mount, South Hermitage and Meole for example; many lawns were dug up and much of the sacred Quarry came under the plough. However, under Parks Superintendent G. S. Ingle, the Dingle, that central showpiece of the Quarry with its scarlet and gold begonias and calceolarias, retained its pre-war attractiveness, and there were always the crocuses in early Spring. There was also the majestic avenue of lime trees – for a time that is, for when in October 1944 the limes were pronounced unsafe, much public disquiet was felt, and when six months later felling actually started, much sadness also.

A trivial matter when seen against the much broader backcloth? There were those who considered Shrewsbury folk too preoccupied with their own petty problems, as exemplified by the reply to a gentleman who had complained of pigeon nuisance in the Square. Were pigeons the worst we had to put up with, he was asked, and the letter continued "My advice to you, sir, is keep your chin up but not under the Shire Hall, as these birds make no exceptions".

However, there was one problem which at the time seemed anything but trivial to those most affected. Would the powers-that-be please drain that part of the old disused Shropshire Union Canal which traversed densely populated Ditherington, residents politely asked, particularly those who lived in New Park Close. New Park Close came to be known as the 'Black Hole of Shrewsbury' on account of the stinking overflow which disgorged itself into the properties there. Would Kingsland tolerate such living conditions, the Chronicle wanted to know. That question was never answered, and it was another eighteen months before the canal was finally emptied, firstly of what many years ago had been water, and then of the dozens of prams, mattresses and other rubbish that lay rotting at the bottom.

Britain's entry into a state of war was a signal to the clerk of the weather to dispatch, in 1939–40 and 1940–41, two of the severest winters of the present century. Hail, snow and frost in January 1940 heralded the Great Freeze, and on the 28th the Severn was dotted with miniature icebergs. The following day a train took ten hours to get from Stoke to Shrewsbury. The subsequent thaw brought flooding, and on 8th

February a woman was drowned downstream from the Kingsland Bridge. However if 1940 was bad. 1941 proved even worse. After snow heavier than most people could remember. many roads were covered to the hedge-tops and there were fifteen-foot drifts at Bayston Hill. Some town premises were shut for days: country bus services ceased altogether. There was also the inevitable flood to look forward to. and expectations of a spectacular one were not disappointed. The figure of eighteen feet represented the highest level since 1869. Of the bridges only Kingland could be crossed. The Quarry was under water nearly to the bandstand: so were seats in the Empire cinema. and there were two feet of it in the Abbey vestry. Frankwell was virtually obliterated. Residents in Abbey Foregate whose houses were inundated. isolating them for two days or more. complained bitterly of the absence of official warnings.

As if to compensate. 1941 brought a brilliant summer. and so did 1942. whereas the following three summers of war were all average to indifferent. But at least there were the long light evenings. Britain was either one or two hours ahead of Greenwich Mean Time between 25th February 1940 and 6th October 1945. continuously. that is. for more than five and a half years. There was no double summer-time in 1940: it was introduced for the months of May. June and July in 1941. brought forward to include April during the next three years. and ended early in 1945. on 15th July.

VE and VJ Days. similar in some respects. were different in this: whereas victory in Europe had long been anticipated and looked forward to. victory in the Far East took most people by surprise. There was also the fact that while VJ Day could be celebrated with the clearest of consciences. many had previously had misgivings about making merry at a time when war still went on and looked like going on for a long while yet.

Before VE Day dawned the Shrewsbury Chronicle commented "When it comes it will be a time for rejoicing but for sober rejoicing: the prevailing mood should be one not of festivity but of thanksgiving". And after it was over: "The official celebrations though full of dignity lacked heartiness". Not so the unofficial ones – a state of affairs that was not universally approved of. A serving soldier wrote home to say that V-Day celebrations were sick-making: this wasn't a picnic: men were still being killed: to talk about celebrating stank. Celebrating there was. nevertheless. The news of Germany's surrender was known on Monday May 7th. although the official announcement by the Prime Minister was delayed until the following day at 3 p.m.. and that evening the King broadcast. In Shrewsbury. festivities that night were centred on the Square. now fully lit once more. where many danced to music from the Old Market Hall. and some climbed Clive's statue. Pride Hill was solid with crowds. Factory sirens sounded. fireworks were let off. flags were flown. Meadow Place boasted a large 'V' in flashing lights. On Wednesday May 9th the rejoicing continued. The KSLI and Frankwell Jazz bands played in the Quarry. Lewis's Ballroom was packed. the statue climbers had moved on to Darwin outside the Library: Pengwern Boat Club lit a bonfire. and at the Sentinel Works an effigy of Hitler was burned. Also it marked the beginning of a string of children's parties in all parts of the borough.

However, a more sober note was struck. Near the entrance to the Quarry, at the base of the Archangel Michael war memorial someone had placed a bunch of red tulips.

Three and a half months afterwards, late on the night of Tuesday August 14th, the surprise came. Rapidly the news spread. Thereafter the night was a warm one in more ways than one. Somehow bonfires got lit. Reported the Chronicle "Girls appeared from nowhere, their hair in curlers and some in their night attire". Robert Clive found himself with a pint mug on his head and later a dustbin lid (and it was a fact that when VJ celebrations were finally over, the number of serviceable dustbin lids in Shrewsbury had noticeably diminished). Although it rained on VJ Day itself few ardours were dampened. Again the Square formed the nucleus of a town in rapturous mood. "People were climbing anything that could be climbed", said the Chronicle. Policemen were dancing like everybody else. Someone asked for a hat to decorate Clive and was presented with a pair of knickers. Outside the American Red Cross Club in Castle Street had been inscribed a sign: 'Well, you good folks, it's all over. Thanks to us all they did not knock the Cliffs of Dover. We will remember you".

In the succeeding days a further round of children's street parties were held. Quite where all the food came from nobody seemed to know, nor did they care. Parties were still going on at the beginning of September, and then suddenly everything was over, and all were wondering was it normality again – at last?

"Dark are the days"

C.D: not always the Corps Diplomatique, as the occasional victim of officiousness might have testified, but Civil Defence; and if the odd Bumble or two were found among its ranks, so were many heroes as well. Sometimes they could even have been the same person. Shrewsbury firemen and police were quickly on the scene after the Coventry raid of November 1940; unsung heroes all – who perhaps are the best sort of heroes after all.

While the country speculated whether Hitler would (uncharacteristically) draw back from the brink, in Shrewsbury shelter trenches began to be dug all over the place, though not without some criticism of the cost. Actual shelters came later; the Home Office did not at first consider them necessary, for was this not a safe area? Sandbags soon became a familiar part of the landscape, first-aid posts were set up, sirens installed, and all pigeon-fanciers were required to register. "Don't put on your respirator until the gas rattle is sounded", each civilian was advised. "We entered upon the conflict better prepared than we were in 1914" stated the leader writer of the Chronicle, although if that were so, in 1914 we must have been in dire peril indeed.

Most schools had their own shelters. The difficulty was whether members of the public should be allowed to use them. Eventually it was decided that they could – out of school hours. At the beginning of January 1940, about the time when Oliver Stanley was succeeding Hore Belisha as War Minister, the Girls' High School in Town Walls was appealing to parents to donate £2 towards the cost of building shelter protection.

Human nature being what it is, as time went by and Shrewsbury did not get blitzed, shelters came to be treated more and more casually. Children played in them; they became unpleasantly damp; by late 1941 there were complaints that their principal benefits seemed to be reserved for gipsies and courting couples. Sandbags, having been filled so dutifully and conscientiously in the first place, in the end often lay mutilated and abandoned. To pretend that Britain was at all points and at all times keyed up to defend herself efficiently is patently futile.

However, our air-raid wardens scarcely deserved the caricature-like treatment they so often received then and which they have gone on receiving ever since. They were doing a job which had necessarily to be either dangerous or monotonous. Organised from ARP headquarters at Porch House, Swan Hill, exercises and practices which in the beginning had at least the virtue of novelty, began to pall. "Some people are getting a little impatient and are wondering when things are going to happen" observed the Shrewsbury Chronicle on 5th April 1940. In the broader sense people had not long to wait, for within the week Denmark and Norway had been invaded ("Not only a crime but a blunder"). But in far-off Shrewsbury things went on much as they had done before.

To keep the ARP service keen and on its toes during long months of inactivity was not easy. Lectures and courses continued to be attended. Directives were issued. In June 1940 appeared a list of DO's and DON'Ts: "If air raiders come DO take cover, stay at home, remove car from street" (in that order?), "avoid windows, let people in, obey. DON'T run risks, be without gas-masks, use telephone unnecessarily, gossip." The following month, when air action was intensifying, more advice was forthcoming: "What do I do when I hear guns, explosions and air-raid warnings? I keep a cool head. I take cover, I gather my family with gas-masks and go quietly to my shelter or refuge room. I do not try to 'have a look'. I do not rush about alarming people. I remember that a lot of noise is good noise – our guns firing at the enemy." The tone, a little redolent of the infants' school, should not be criticised too harshly.

Air attacks on Shropshire were virtually confined to that summer of 1940. In June five bombs were dropped at Shawbury, and in July ten at Tern Hill, but no-one was hurt; however, on 31st August Shrewsbury suffered its only air-raid casualties of the war when a lone raider dropped an incendiary and two high-explosives, killing three occupants of a cottage opposite the old river bed on Ellesmere Road. In September 1939 a Public Assistance Commission had been set up to provide food and accommodation for the victims of air-raids, although not until March 1941 did a War Damage bill become law. Inquests were not normally held on deaths from air-raids.

Surprisingly, during that tense and fateful summer of 1940 a serious shortage of wardens was reported. Three months later, at the time when the London blitz was at its height, new regulations were issued: the first siren was now an alert only, and work was to proceed until a futher warning was given. ARP and 'siren' jokes were becoming current, as exemplified by the following: "Take cover, you fool, can't you hear the siren?" "Yes, I heard it but it ain't nowt to do with me, I come from Wenlock and that's the siren I has to listen for."

1939, 1940 and to a lesser extent 1941 were the most active years for Shrewsbury ARP. Thereafter, although discipline was kept up and duties were faithfully observed, routine had taken over from innovation. It was scarcely any fault of theirs that not all of the volunteers were called upon to risk their lives in the cause of freedom.

On 11th August 1945 on Shrewsbury School playing field a farewell parade of Civil Defence personnel took place. No fewer than 1,400 attended it.

"Dark are the days through which we grope," began one of those patriotic poems which wars seem to inspire. Nothing like as dark as the nights, one might have retorted, unless one's home happened to be in Harlescott or Monkmoor, those two suburbs having gained the reputation of being the worst offenders against black-out regulations. With the war less than a fortnight old, the owner of a fish shop in Coleham (not known as chippies in those days) had the unhappy distinction of paying the first fine (£2) for a lighting infringement. He was by no means the last. So widespread an offence did it turn out to be and one taken so seriously by the magistrates that by August 1940, when air-raids in the Midlands were starting, they warned that fining could be superseded by imprisonment. However, in their mercy they were moved to withhold that particular punishment from Shrewsbury's Town Clerk (no less) when he made an unfortunate appearance before them. He was able to blame his maid! Nevertheless he was still fined, as was the lady who claimed that she had turned her light on while sleep-walking.

Strangers to the town and newcomers were not always impressed by the state of the town's precautions. In December 1940 a Birmingham visitor was critical, while the following month a Londoner wrote "I have lived in several towns since the war commenced but never in one where the residents treat the black-out with the calm indifference like they do in Shrewsbury."

Of course in one sense the more total the compliance with regulations the more dangerous conditions were, and ironically the black-out turned out to be a greater hazard than the air-raids it was designed to prevent. In Shrewsbury the river, which virtually encircles the town, was a particular peril. The war was scarcely a fortnight old before the first road death occurred: a man killed by a bus in blacked-out Barker Street. 'Look out in the black-out' became the slogan, and a necessary one too, for in the country as a whole, in one month of December 1939, no fewer than 1,200 died in the darkness. Pedestrians were vulnerable; so were cyclists. Wear something white, they were told, but sighted persons were requested not to carry white sticks. Probably only those who experienced the black-out can appreciate the burden of it; in spite of the jokes of the 'overheard in the black-out' variety ("Be guided by me, Colonel") its effect was to induce depression and despondency.

"I think that when we look back on this war period we shall regard the black-out as one of our worst trials" wrote 'The Guvnor' (Shrewsbury Chronicle) on 28th February 1941. Yet not for another two years was there to be any lifting of restrictions, and then only in the case of buses and trains, and not until September 1944 (when most people thought the war in Europe would be over by Christmas) was there any appreciable relaxation. Street lighting could now be increased, the only trouble being that the necessary fittings were not actually available; and housewives were permitted to hang ordinary curtains, if they had any to hang or were able to get some, which did not necessarily follow.

The idea of having roof watchers to pinpoint the activities of enemy aircraft and if practicable to put out incendiaries seems to have been born in the late Summer of 1940, and in November we hear of a lady being appointed to instruct volunteers in the art of roof spotting. Whether not enough volunteers came forward is uncertain, but it was not until the scheme became modified and people were not necessarily required to go up on roofs that it caught on. The Ministry of Home Security Fire Watchers Order decreed that where firms had more than thirty employees and/or occupied 50,000 cubic feet of space, a fire watcher had always to be on the premises. Fires did not rage in Shrewsbury, nevertheless for a while fire watching became all the rage, and not only where it was compulsory. There were even areas such as Kingsland and Port Hill where fire parties were formed to look after groups of houses, the whole operation taking on certain social connotations. But it was a serious job for all that. It was given out that the fire watcher who really knew his business needed to carry or be able to lay his hands on no fewer than eighteen items of equipment including a long-handled shovel under one arm, a rake under the other, spare sand in his pockets and a wet blanket round his neck!

In 1940 attack from the air was not the only form of offensive in people's minds. Throughout the summer of that year the talk was of invasion; indeed it was regarded as a near certainty, and in May the LDV (Local Defence Volunteers) was formed, with its headquarters at 2 Claremont Buildings and Brigadier W. R. H. Dann as its first commanding officer. Within five minutes of the wireless announcement of its formation the first volunteer had presented himself at the police station in Swan Hill, and from then on recruitment was swift. Not known as the Home Guard until the following August they were first nicknamed the Parashooters, paratroop invasion scares being rife at the time. Anything and everything, including hay swirling in the wind, was mistaken for descending parachutists in that summer of 1940, and when the hay harvest was in, it was stacked in the middle of fields to obstruct landing aircraft. Public ridicule of the Home Guard was no invention of the script writers of 'Dad's Army'. There were complaints at the time of the old men running LDV's, and as late as 1943 a letter from an army officer referred to them as "those decrepit old gentlemen". Nevertheless they were appreciated by some. "When people keep going for four years long after the novelty has worn off, it's a good sign," wrote 'The Guvnor' in May 1944, and that same writer at the end of the war advised Shrewsbury servicemen "When you come home don't think you've done it all; the old man has done his bit in a modest way."

Once the immediate threat of invasion was over, much of the excitement was over also, to be followed by routine parades, inspections and training. The sinking of HMS Hood and the British withdrawal from Crete in the summer of 1941 were signalled in Shrewsbury by a large-scale defence exercise. Civilians were advised to stay indoors. Street blocks were set up, tear gas used. Eighteen members of the public who had the temerity to venture out were found to be without identity cards; however, one old lady was wiser. She kept hers in her stocking. "That's the only safe place to keep it at my age" she explained.

Command of the 1st Battalion Home Guard passed to Major F. H. Liddell in January 1942, but by then its purpose too was passing, and at Easter of the following year the bells of Shrewsbury's churches, reserved during darker days for warning of invasion, were rung for only the second time since the fall of France. Towards the end of 1944 rumours were circulating that the Home Guard was to stand down and that all ranks were soon to enjoy a lie-in on a Sunday morning. For once a rumour was true. Stand-down (not disbandment) was fixed for Sunday 3rd December, coincidentally at a time when away to the east its counterpart in Germany was being born. After a service at St. Chad's, six hundred marched to Barker Street. The band played 'There'll always be an England' and, as the Shrewsbury Chronicle reporter put it, "the men broke away from what will probably be their last parade, and dispersed". For four and a half years the Home Guard, described as the least expensive fighting force in history, had commanded loyalties of an uncommon sort.

An important role in the defence system was played by the regular police and the 'specials' under successive Chief Constables Frank Davies, G. H. Macdivitt and T. E. Barnwell. Vital, too, were the Observer Corps and the Fire Service; besides Coventry, Shrewsbury firemen also provided much-needed assistance during air-raids on Birmingham. Amidst the town, and encircling it, roared, droned, rumbled those various army and air force units which were a part of everyday life yet at the same time above and beyond it: the KSLI at Copthorne, the Parachute Regiment at Shelton, RAF Monkmoor and so on. Shawbury's aeroplanes guarded in the imagination, if not in fact, the skies above Shrewsbury – aeroplanes from No. 11 Flying Training School (later No. 11 Pilots' Advanced Flying Unit) and later from the Empire Air Navigation School.

But Air Commodore N. H. D'eath, Shawbury's commanding officer, and all the other pilots and navigators who flew from his station, were not the only fliers who helped defend Britain from attack and later carried the war into enemy-held territory. One day in February 1943, at Maddox's in Pride Hill, a rather special and unusual show took place. There, at a time when the Russian victory at Stalingrad was being celebrated, customers were invited to meet and pay their respects to a character by the name of Beachcomber whose exploits had included carrying vital dispatches from the raid on Dieppe. For Beachcomber the pigeon, it must have been a very proud day indeed.

"Picking holes in each other will not help to win the war"

... an entirely reasonable sentiment, uttered by R. J. P. – a correspondent to the Shrewsbury Chronicle on 20th August 1943. Picking holes will not help to win wars or very much else for that matter, but usually that does not prevent people from picking them. How did the war affect Salopians' attitudes to their fellow creatures, to human beings near and far? How did they cope with the advent of new neighbours and new influences? How react to tensions heretofore unsuspected, now experienced for the first time?

To look initially at what ought ideally to be a stabilising force in the field of human relations, it must be said that the attitude of Shrewsbury's churches in the Second World War differed markedly from that of 1914–18. Then the clergy had been militant in the extreme. Now a milder tone altogether prevailed; in theatrical terms they had moved upstage. In their churches and chapels the emphasis was less on chauvinistic fulminations from the pulpits, more on worship at the altars. It made a welcome change.

The outbreak of war brought only a few alterations to the pattern of public worship. In winter, in some cases, evening services became afternoon ones; church halls were given over to entertaining the troops; national days of prayer were observed periodically. Battle of Britain Sunday was instituted during the war and not, as might be supposed, after it. High Street Unitarian Church had its 250th anniversary, St. Chad's its 150th, and Bishop Moriarty (the Roman Catholic Bishop of Shrewsbury) his Golden Jubilee. There were Jewish services at St. Catherine's Hall, Corporation Lane; Radbrook Church in Kenwood Drive was opened. The Reverend Kenneth Slack, later a well-known figure in religious broadcasting, officiated at St. Nicholas' Presbyterian in Castle Gates. The Reverend L. Newby (vicar of St. Julian's since 1916) retired, and C. B. Roach, who preceded W. A. Parker and Forbes Horan at St. Chad's, was heard to deprecate the intelligentsia as exemplified by H. G. Wells "who have no belief and who have warped minds, who cannot understand the human side of people." To be fair, bias of this sort was the exception, not the rule. Indeed, bearing in mind most ex-cathedra pronouncements during the First War, bishops during the Second were a fairly radical bunch. It was during the later war that Shrewsbury welcomed its first Anglican suffragan bishop, E. K. C. Hamilton; the second, Bishop Hodson, was among the first to protest against the dropping of the atom bomb. Here he was following the example of his superior at Lichfield, Dr. E. S. Woods. Woods was a gentle, saintly man, whose appeal to his flock was always for a spirit of mercy, pity and forgiveness, a stance which in its turn resembled that of Archbishop Temple of Canterbury. Shortly after D-Day the Archbishop preached to a congregation of 1,500 in Shrewsbury's St. Mary's, and later visited Normandy casualties in the R.S.I. He differed from Woods in that he was very much a political bishop who deplored the unequal distribution of wealth and the sanctity of the profit motive. Then there was Bishop Bell of Chichester who, like Woods, opposed saturation bombing. Sabre rattling among the clergy generally was not common between 1939 and 1945.

With regard to cordiality between the denominations bishops, priests and ministers were probably some distance ahead of their flocks; entrenched attitudes among their congregations precluded any real ecumenical advance. Woods of Lichfield was actually the first Anglican bishop to be received in audience by the Pope (in August 1944), and three years earlier in Shrewsbury Castle church leaders, including Roman Catholics, had shared a platform to discuss the Pope's five peace points in an atmosphere of fellowship and friendliness. But these were only small steps forward; generally Catholic-Protestant distrust remained strong. Declared Mr. Thomas Forrester of Yorton Heath "If I had to choose between Roman Catholicism and Bolshevism I would choose the latter as the lesser evil", and these thoughts were by no means unrepresentative.

Shrewsbury's capacity for tolerance and forbearance was tested to the full immediately on the outbreak of war, for after all there is nothing like having strangers in your home for raising the blood pressure and pinching the nerves. The town was to experience further influxes of evacuees – a minor wave in 1941, and again in 1944 at the time of the flying bomb attacks on London – but nothing to compare with the major invasion of September 1939, when many thousands of schoolchildren were absorbed into local life: absorbed or else left stranded on its surface, insoluble and infusible.

They came by train from Merseyside, mothers with young children, older ones on their own, youngsters of all sizes and conditions. There were pupils from Liverpool's Holt High School and Queen Mary's High who shared a double-shift system with the two Priory Schools. There were girls from Belvidere and Birkenhead High to be fitted in at Shrewsbury High School; South Church, Bishop Goss, All Souls Walton, Old Swan, St. Catherine's Edgehill were other Merseyside schools to descend on the town in those early days of the war; and Monkmoor, Coleham, St. George's and the resurrected Trinity (Belle Vue) were among those Shrewsbury schools soon to resound with accents that were quite unfamiliar, for the fact is that with their homes a mere sixty miles apart, the children of Liverpool and of Shrewsbury knew no more of one another's background and way of life than if they had inhabited different planets.

Host families were "expected to care for (evacuees) as if they were their own" and Holt School reciprocated by publicly thanking the citizens of Shrewsbury for "their good services and hospitality." When Christmas came, evidence of that hospitality was conspicuous in the shape of parties throughout the town.

Was it a matter then of sweetness and light all round? No, unfortunately. In the first place the allowance of 10/6 a week for the first child and 8/6 for each additional one was found by many housewives to be inadequate, a situation exacerbated by the fact that hosts often had to provide clothes for their guests (medical treatment was paid for by the government), and sometimes by the children's parents expecting free meals when visiting their offspring. One lady complained of being regarded by such parents "as a kind of lodging-house keeper".

Dissatisfaction on the part of many of the newcomers, too, soon became apparent, and as early as 8th September the Shrewsbury Chronicle was reporting "the return of a number of adult evacuees who were unable to accustom themselves to rural conditions. . . they expected that there would be trams or frequent bus services, and the lack of fish and chip shops is also mentioned as a grievance". By the 15th many mothers and young children had departed, disillusioned, and a week later one young evacuee stole a bicycle and pedalled home to Birkenhead on it. The Reverend Eric Treacy, vicar of St. Mary's Edgehill, felt constrained to point out some of the more unpalatable facts of life as he was used to seeing them: slum children did not respect law and order, they were used to different food, they swore and so on, and certainly some evacuees provided the more conventional of Shrewsbury's citizens with shocks. At a county conference the following March, plans for further evacuation schemes were received coldly in view of recent experiences. "A considerable number of the people evacuated were in a dirty and infectious condition and their personal habits were in some cases deplorable" it was stated. However, by that time the worst was over. There were fewer evacuees about, and many who remained were in the process of being turned into Salopians. Other gains there were. Many sincere thanks were expressed, and when Holt School returned home they presented the Boys' Priory with a house rugby cup in gratitude. Some, too, might detect pathos as well as satisfaction in the words of a letter written by young evacuee Kenneth Taylor: "I have had a wonderful time since I came to Shropshire. I did not know there could be such lovely scenery. I did not know there could be so much sky. I'm sure there was not nearly so much, and it was usually grey, at Liverpool."

Observers might have been forgiven for supposing on occasions that the war being fought on an international scale was of smaller significance than the civil one going on within the borough boundaries. Like the Wars of the Roses, the Great Billeting Controversy flared up intermittently over a long period, and now and again aroused great heat.

It was a problem that ran parallel to that of the evacuee children. The war created a population shift. Firms and departments moved from one part of the country to another, the bombed-out sought shelter in safer areas, thousands of servicemen (and sometimes their wives too) were billeted privately. It would have been surprising had everything gone smoothly.

The campaign ran thus: one side attacked, whereupon defences were hastily mustered on the other; later the roles might be reversed. Meanwhile there were pacifiers trying to instil sense into both parties and put affairs into perspective.

The autumn of 1940 seems to have been a particularly trying time. Newcomers with babies were finding it hard to get accommodation anywhere. Prices asked did not always seem reasonable. One desperate lady from London wrote "I suggested (to the authorities) that there were very few people in the large houses on Kingsland and was told that district is reserved!!! I suppose they know the richer people do not want strangers in their houses. I can assure you it is just as painful for us to go into other people's homes – especially when you know you are not wanted. Shrewsbury does not seem to realise we are at war. The clergy who know their flock should impress upon them it is their duty to give help. I do not wish Shrewsbury folk any harm but I should like them one and all to spend a week in London which is the front line".

The denials and counter-charges were immediate. Newcomers would be welcome if they were prepared to do for themselves. Profiteering was not going on. "How" wrote one Salopian, "can householders be expected to welcome into their houses (which sometimes contain valuables) people of whom they know nothing except that they come from London which can hardly be regarded as a certificate as to character." A London girl was heard to complain about having to wait on herself in digs. Could there be more co-operation by guests, came the reply, rather than their just regarding the place as lodgings?

Happier were the testimonials. "I commend to you this flower of Salop. Cherish it." And this from an AC2 who, finishing his letter "What wouldn't I give to be back in Shrewsbury now?", paid this sincerest of tributes: "Always I was treated as though I were a son of the family. . ."

Self-righteousness is a human failing at any time; in war-time we seem particularly vulnerable to it. Blame, it seems, has to be meted out, and scapegoats found, for our own ease of mind and, apparently, our justification. Nor are the enemy always the prime target. During World War Two men exempted from military service ("skulking pansies" one letter in the Chronicle called them), tramps who "should not be allowed to wander about the country doing nothing," those doing no war work, strikers – yes, strikers – all came in for condemnation. We think of strikes as a manifestation of current degeneracy, but 80,000 miners came out in March 1944, London underground workers later did the same, as did Midland Red employees. There was also a dockers' go-slow.

Officially, conscientious objectors were treated less hysterically than in 1914–18, but prison sentences were still passed, and the judgement of the public less than generous; less than rational too, in some cases. Said one councillor, in favour of dismissing Shrewsbury's council staff who were CO's, "While the law allows people to become CO's it does not say the local government shall provide sanctuary for them". Another affirmed that he did not understand the mentality of CO's, it seemed to be a clear case of whether a man was British or not. Another gentleman took exception to their being allowed to teach in schools, in fact he put the rise in crime down to it. Many soldiers had been religious, pointed out yet another opponent of conscientious objectors, apparently under the impression that he had adduced a telling argument; while an education committee member reasoned that mixed schools were more likely to produce CO's. "If I had a dozen sons" he said, "the first thing I would consider in choosing a school for them was: will they be taught to become men?"

British superiority over foreign races (especially those of darker skin) was taken for granted. If they happened to be dark and also hostile to British interests, contempt was magnified, and so it follows, firstly, that on the world scene no one person was despised more than Gandhi, and secondly, that in a specifically war setting the Italians were seen in a less favourable light than our German adversaries. From 1943 especially, Italian prisoners-of-war in their brown-patched suits became a familiar sight in the fields round Shrewsbury, and an ironic little incident occurred when a number of them on a country road were scattered by a bus bearing the sign 'Montgomery'. They were generally considered pampered. The amount of liberty allowed them was disapproved of, so that when Italian workers at Allscott went on strike in October 1944 one serving soldier was impelled to write: "We were disgusted to read about these well-fed, greasy, lazy, impudent foreigners having the cheek to go on strike. . . if I was behind these macaroni pushers there wouldn't have been any strike".

German POW's, detested though they might be, were never seen in quite that way. The martial spirit of Nazi Germany was easily feared but less easily despised, and while the usual eccentric opinions could be heard – for example that German music had little merit and should not be played – anti-German feeling was much less violent than it had been (with less justification) in the earlier war. Where patriotic poems in 1914–18 had poured out invective against the 'Hun', in World War Two it was much more likely to be high ideals such as freedom that were apostrophised. The debate which was held between Shrewsbury School and the Girls' High School in July 1945 ('that patriotism is a vice rather than a virtue') could not feasibly have taken place thirty years earlier.

For those old friends and allies whom Germany had over-run – Poles, Czechs, Dutch and so on – Shrewsbury's feelings were manifestly warm. A cosmopolitan town for the first and probably the last time, Shrewsbury had a local branch of the Friends of the Fighting French, and Maddox's exhibition of paintings under the auspices of the French Committee for National Liberation enjoyed a packed opening. Jewish refugees had a sympathetic reception, while enthusiasm for Russia's cause was exemplified by the formation in the borough of an Anglo-Soviet Unity Committee. Beethoven, Schumann, Wagner might safely be ignored; the darling of the music lovers was now Tchaikovsky.

Finally, what of the Americans? Research suggests that today's recollection of the average G.I. as "overpaid, over-sexed and over here" is something of an exaggeration, and after all Shrewsbury ought to know, for it saw sufficient of them, over roughly a three-year period, to judge.

While few of us would endorse that letter writer to the Shrewsbury Chronicle who in October 1940 beseeched "May we be inspired by such great spiritual leaders as President Roosevelt", there were many ways in which the arrival of real (as distinct from Hollywood) Americans benefited local society. "Most people get used to the English climate eventually", sanguinely declared the US services handbook, but truly Shrewsbury folk got used to having Americans in their midst much more quickly than that. They came in 1942, and that winter their fleecy-lined jackets were both admired and envied. Apart from smart clothes an asset they did not lack was generosity. Gifts and visits by them to the Royal Salop Infirmary and the Eye, Ear and Throat Hospital, and a children's party at the Granada provided out of their own money and rations, marked Christmas 1942, and many habitually gave their sweet rations to Shrewsbury children. "Got any gum, chum?" and "Lend us a penny" became familiar cries, and ones which reflected more credit on those addressed than on those who uttered them.

For those readers who remember the Raven Hotel in Castle Street (now the site of Woolworths), from April 1943 until the end of the war it became the American Red Cross Club, flying the Stars and Stripes; appropriately it was officially opened on 4th July with "a tea party very different from the unhappy affair at Boston in 1773". On its first anniversary Ben Russak, the club's first director (and friend of Humphrey Bogart), had this to say: "This club has proved that Anglo-American co-operation is a fact and that it works... the American soldiers' introduction to the best which Britain has to offer exists in this club... to the people of Shrewsbury we say thanks a million".

In May 1944 Russak was appointed director of the Mayflower Club in London's Edgware Road, but the same spirit of friendliness seems to have prevailed under his successors, Hermione Santhoff, and later R. S. Phillips. The club proved to be no enclave. Its members fully joined in the social and sporting life of the town. Table tennis and darts were taken up, and local sides met. Baseball and American football were witnessed at the County Ground and Gay Meadow. In the summer of 1944 a certain Staff Sergeant Joe Louis gave exhibitions of boxing. The following Christmas one hundred and fifty children were entertained to dinner and games at the American's Atcham base.

Because Americans enjoyed superior facilities to those of the British servicemen, some envy was inevitable. One soldier contrasted the American club "a smart hotel with lounges, games rooms and every other commodity, selling steak and chips, and even seats outside in the sun with all the latest papers and magazines", with "our own club across the road (the Red Shield at 32 Castle Street), a dingy old shop selling rock cakes and tea". One can agree – it didn't seem fair. Local hostility had been aroused also when, late in 1943, Sergeant Michael Pilhosh was court-martialled for the murder on 9th September, near the Wrekin's Forest Glen, of ATS Private Louisa Price. Pilhosh was acquitted, and for a while public feeling ran high, but it wasn't long before the special relationship had sailed into calmer waters again.

For representatives of a people not at that time renowned for its cordiality to other nationalities, Shrewsbury's reception of its American allies was greatly to its credit. New friends were acquired, and often (in the case of local girls) husbands. "I am convinced that we will never forget Shrewsbury" wrote the club's last director when it finally closed down on 15th August 1945 – a classic case, surely, of the happy ending.

MISS LIGHTFOOT works in a factory all day. She makes no song or dance about it, but she is doing her bit. And the thing you couldn't help noticing is that even in wartime conditions she is seldom tired, never ill, never nervy. What is it Miss Lightfoot does that perhaps you dont? She eats potatoes and carrots. So do you. But *she* eats them every day—and every day in a different way. They protect her from illness and fatigue and keep her full of vitality. They'll do just the same for you.

Carrot Sandwiches for a change

1. Add two parts of grated raw carrot to one part of finely shredded white heart of cabbage, and bind with chutney or sweet pickle. Pepper and salt to taste.

2. Equal amounts of grated raw carrot, cabbage heart and crisp celery bound with chutney or sweet pickle. Pepper and salt to taste.

3. Bind some grated raw carrot with mustard sauce, flavoured with a dash of vinegar.

4. Cook diced carrot in curry sauce until tender enough to spread easily with a knife.

All these fillings taste their best with wholemeal bread.

Our dockers don't mind risking their lives to unload your food, but if you waste it their language is something horrible !

"Fadge" for Breakfast

"Fadge" is both nourishing and filling. It is excellent for breakfast.

Boil some well-scrubbed potatoes, then peel and mash them while hot. When the mixture is cool enough to handle, add salt, and work in enough flour to make a pliable dough. Knead lightly on a well floured board for about 5 minutes, then roll into a large circle about ¼ in. thick. Cut into wedge shaped pieces and cook on a hot girdle, an electric hot-plate or on the upper shelf of a quick oven until brown on both sides, turning once.

Carrot-Cap Salad

Every woman who values her good complexion should have this salad regularly.

Cook two or three good sized potatoes in their skins. When tender, strain without drying off, to avoid making them floury. Slice and dice neatly; then dress in vinaigrette dressing (two parts of salad oil to one of vinegar, pepper and salt to taste) while they are still hot. Pile in a salad bowl lined with a few shredded lettuce leaves or watercress. Sprinkle with a little chopped chive or rings of spring onion, and pile high with grated carrot.

Potato Floddies

These are real energy givers.

Scrub 2 potatoes and grate with a coarse grater over a bowl. Then add sufficient flour to form a batter. Season with salt and pepper. Melt a little dripping and make very hot in a frying pan. Drop the mixture into it. When brown on one side, turn and brown on the other. Serve with a little jam if you want it as a sweet dish. If you want it as a savoury, add a pinch of mixed herbs and a dash of cayenne pepper.

When you "dig for victory," grow vegetables that will store for Winter and Spring use, such as potatoes, carrots, and onions.

FOOD IS A MUNITION OF WAR

DON'T WASTE IT

Remember to turn on your wireless at 8.15 every morning for useful food tips from the radio Kitchen Front.

"Grow more greens and keep away the blues"

Food rationing, administered by the Ministry of Food firstly from Claremont Hill, then after July 1942 from Swan Hill Court, began as a gradual process in December 1939, and although people grumbled, and although the size of ration of the various staple foodstuffs tended to diminish as the war progressed, agreement is widespread that British children were better nourished at the end of the war than they had been before it.

Strangely, despite the awfulness of trying to shop in those days, the most popular government Minister among housewives was probably Lord Woolton, who became Food Minister in April 1940, and few were pleased when he was moved to Post-War Planning three and half years later. Woolton it was who mobilised the nation's women 'on the kitchen front', bringing imagination and even humour to the job. Wonderful were the recipes and food hints which emanated from his Ministry: new ways with cabbages, grated carrot sandwich ("a fine sustainer for an energetic child"), potato and watercress soup, Shropshire salad; there was even a festive quiz, Father being required to deduct five from his score in the event of his having kept his Christmas sweet ration for himself.

The aforementioned dish, Shropshire salad, was just one consequence of Shrewsbury's 'Dig for Victory' campaign, in which allotments were frenziedly dug and the Quarry itself ploughed up. The Shrewsbury Chronicle gave a cup for the best vegetable plot. The mayor, Harry Steward, declared that schoolboys ought to learn gardening before Latin, and such well-known figures as Freddie Grisewood, C. H. Middleton and Frank Phillips came to the town to take part in brains-trusts and to speak in the cause. Truly, allotmentitis had taken a firm grip:

> "For we're fed up with your trickery
> And we'll dig like smoke for victory,
> We're after you, Herr Adolf, with a spade."

Thus concluded the Marching Song of the Victory Diggers, composed after a 'Dig for Victory' meeting at the Castle on 8th February 1941, a meeting which also generated two eye-catching slogans: 'Grow more greens and keep away the blues" and "Cultivation may save the nation." Maddox's, always to the fore in any propaganda exercise, did much to encourage that cultivation. Besides devoting advertising space to it ('Forget about the Second Front and concentrate on that Second Vegetable' appeared in time for Easter 1944), they maintained their own two and a quarter acres in Salts Field near Kingland Bridge and a demonstration allotment near the swimming baths. Schools, too, dug away merrily, while the borough council provided free manure for anyone who was prepared to collect it.

The council's own allotments were able to provide vegetables for the St. Michael's Street British Restaurant when it opened its doors on Monday 10th August 1942. Although a municipal undertaking, the British Restaurant was required to be selfsupporting. Improbably, lunches at one shilling and twopence enabled the books to be balanced, and the enterprise continued to flourish not only until the end of the war but for a period after it.

SHROPSHIRE SALAD

A recipe for a delicious, easy-to-make salad that will tempt the whole family

Shropshire Salad tastes even more delightful than it sounds!

Begin by lining your salad bowl with greenstuffs. For this, you can use lettuce separated into leaves, or shredded raw cabbage, and sprigs of watercress. Spinach can also be used, shredded raw (naturally, you'll be sure it's absolutely clean).

It doesn't really matter which of these greens you use, because they're all rich in vitamins and minerals. But cabbage, watercress and spinach are particularly rich in the important Vitamin C, which we're missing at present from fresh fruit. *Raw* vegetables are especially valuable because Vitamin C is reduced by cooking. In fact, a salad a day is more effective than an apple in keeping the doctor away!

Mixing the ingredients

Having arranged the greens, pile in the centre a mixture of diced cooked potatoes, made as follows: Boil 1½ lb. of potatoes in their skins, allow to cool, peel and cut into squares. Then mix the diced potato in a bowl with salad dressing (see recipe below), chopped mint and chopped chives or spring onions.

Arrange a border of cooked diced carrots, beetroots or swedes round the potato and sprinkle the potato with chopped parsley or finish with a tuft of mustard and cress. And there you are!

HOME-MADE SALAD CREAM

This salad cream is easily made. You require: 2 heaped tablespoons dried milk; 1 level teaspoon salt; 1 teaspoon mustard; 2-3 shakes pepper; 2 tablespoons malt vinegar; 1 tablespoon water. Mix all the dry ingredients, add the vinegar and water and beat till a smooth creamy consistency. Serve immediately.

Keep greenstuffs fresh by putting in a saucepan, covering with a lid, and standing on a cool floor.

NEW RATION BOOKS

You won't get your new ration book quickly unless the particulars on your present ration book and identity card are correct. If the name, address and National Registration Number are not the same on both, take them to the Food Office at once.

A SALAD
~~An apple~~ a day
keeps the doctor away

THIS IS WEEK 42—THE SECOND WEEK OF RATION PERIOD No. 11
(May 2nd to May 29th)

THE MINISTRY OF FOOD, LONDON, W.I. FOOD FACTS No. 149

Charges. It is intended to make the following charges on opening the Restaurant:—

Soup	1d.
Meat	3d.
Meat Pie	6d.
Potatoes	2d.
Second Vegetable	2d.
Sweet	3d.
Tea or Coffee	1d.

It will be seen that a full meal of soup meat and two vegetables, sweet and tea or coffee will cost 1/-. Prices will be reduced if experience shows this to be possible. Patrons may make up a meal of such portions as they wish. There will always be alternative dishes.

The war also marked the beginning of what was to develop into the School Meals Service, with Harlescott and Monkmoor schools pioneering that particular venture. One member of staff remarked that he felt less like a teacher than a restaurant manager. At the same time the better-off who could afford to eat out regularly in hotels were commonly felt to be taking an unfair advantage.

Similarly with those with lots of time to spare for queueing. To procure the best of what was going in unrationed goods one needed time and patience; but it was a habit that could quickly become an obsession. Queue-itis was defined as the inability to resist joining any string of people whether they were waiting to buy tomatoes or use a public convenience. For practical purposes the early-in-the-week shoppers tended to be the luckiest; also the early morning ones, before the foragers from Wellington and Oakengates (so it was rumoured among Shrewsbury folk) arrived on the scene. Many imported eatables (oranges and lemons, for example) simply vanished from the shops, while fish, potatoes, eggs, cakes exemplified the ones which disappeared and appeared at unpredictable intervals. Also beer and cigarettes, and they too contributed to the fund of apocrypha which grew up in relation to queueing and shortages. A certain Shrewsbury tobacconist, arriving to open up his shop, was promptly sent to the back of the queue! Another who put up a notice 'Closed for stocktaking' found 'Not a long job?' scrawled underneath.

Prices generally rose throughout the war, though hardly at the rate to which inflation has accustomed us today. 1940 saw two budgets, and tax increases which included income tax up to 8/6 in the £, 20% purchase tax on luxuries and 12% on necessities. Some profiteering went on in goods the prices of which were not controlled; there were always people prepared to queue for salmon at 10/- a pound who wouldn't have dreamed of buying it when it was easy to get at 3/6. But rationing undoubtedly helped the less well-off, and there were benefits to be obtained including free milk for babies – the letters of application for which provided yet another source of apocrypha: for example "I have a boy of 18 months, thanking you for same" or "I have a baby of 2 months and did not know anything about it till the milkman told me".

Clothes rationing, introduced in the summer of 1941, came as a surprise to most men and a severe shock to most women. It gave rise to such lamentations on the subject of clothing coupons as the following:

"Coat and frock take twenty-two.
Ten more for a blouse or two.
Half a dozen pairs of stockings
Use up twelve, it's simply shocking.
Then a mack in case it's wet,
Fourteen coupons more, you bet.
An apron and a pair of shoes,
Three and five I now must use.
Dash it, that makes sixty-six –
Nothing left for cami-knicks".

Men could do without double-breasted suits, or turn-ups, or pocket flaps, but the plight of their womenfolk was dire. Hats were replaced by head scarves. Girls were reduced to painting their legs and using eyebrow pencil for seams, and when the Abbey ward held a fete in September 1944 the winner of the beauty contest was presented with – a pair of silk stockings. By the end of the war matters if anything had got worse. Clothes were in short supply and the quality was, in general, poor. A recently demobbed member of the ATS, complaining of the shoddiness of items available, invited the retort that unlike the services this was what civilians had had to put up with all along. "We are all getting shabbier and shabbier" admitted 'The Guvnor' (Shrewsbury Chronicle), and morale was none the better for it.

Petrol had been rationed from the start. Solid fuel was subject to periodic shortages. On the Fuel Controller's office door at the back of the Library (the Free Library as it was then known) appeared the inscription 'Fire Prevention Officer' – which prompted the only possible comment, 'Exactly!'

On the move

One way in which the war affected people's daily lives was the manner in which they were enabled to travel from place to place. Trains, bus services, private motoring were all modes of transport that suffered disruptions – disruptions that met with public disapproval to the extent that nothing throughout the war was more complained about, was more a source of irritation.

The railways may quickly be disposed of. Grievances here were more generalised: to do with curtailed passenger services, the withdrawal of cheap tickets, crowded and uncomfortable carriages, badly lit stations and scant courtesy. More specific, more localised vexations centred on travelling round the immediate area, and here strictures were well-defined and distinctly clamorous.

Nervousness may have had something to do with it, for while traffic density was not high, road casualties were, although it is true that they had started to get fewer by 1942. Certain counter-measures were introduced, including one-way traffic systems in Pride Hill, Mardol and Claremont Street. However, attempts to make the Horsefair side of Abbey Foregate one-way had to be abandoned in the face of fierce local opposition. Meanwhile just outside the town, that stretch of the by-pass from Meole to Emstrey must have presented an extraordinary sight from late 1943 onwards. Closed to traffic until after the end of the war, the military used it as a storage depot for vehicles – up to 1,500 of them it was estimated. There was much impatience to see it restored to its rightful use, and its eventual re-opening on Saturday, 22nd September 1945 took on ceremonial significance with the mayor heading a motorcade. All that was needed now was that north-south by-pass, first widely talked about during this period. Forty years on it is still being talked about.

One result of petrol rationing was to encourage a return to less sophisticated forms of transport, although the trend towards horse-drawn traffic which began after the outbreak of war failed to gain momentum. Cycling, on the other hand, did. There were drawbacks of course – cyclists were vulnerable in the black-out; if their lights were too bright they found themselves in trouble, if not bright enough, again they were at risk; batteries were hard to get. Bicycle stealing became a popular pastime, so that November 1942 saw the police paraphrasing Jack Warner's catch-phrase with a 'Mind your bike' campaign. But in spite of the disadvantages, cycling remained patriotic, healthy and fashionable. Even the mayor rode his bike to work, and when a Red Cross ball took place at Copthorne Barracks on 13th January 1943 one of the inducements held out by the organisers was a free cycle park! A photograph in the Shrewsbury Chronicle of 3rd May 1940 shows workers leaving the Sentinel Works on the Whitchurch Road. All have bikes. There is not a car in sight.

But note: the year was 1940, when the real war began and the fire of patriotism burned with strength and ebullience and when to hoard petrol was not only illegal but a shameful offence. Slowly, subtly the climate changed. At Whitsuntide 1941 the A5 to North Wales was thick with cars, although those who could not afford £125 for a 1938 Hillman Minx or even £55 for a 1936 Standard Nine (typical second-hand prices at the time) were less happy. There was a spate of complaints of petrol being wasted. One vigilant citizen counted twenty-five cars outside a pub. and later the Shrewsbury Chronicle's 'Guvnor' commented "If a man can't walk to the pub for his evening medicine he can't be in great need of it". By April 1942 town car parks suggested to one observer an era not of war but prosperity. and council officials in the habit of using their cars for going home to lunch found that the habit had not gone unnoticed by less fortunate members of the public. Turning to other sections of the community. and again quoting from 'The Guvnor''s weekly column: "Shopping by car nowadays (early 1943) is almost confined to the wives of clergymen who seem to be generously treated by the petrol controller. and of course to the farmers who always appear to be well-off for juice". Six months later H. Harper was writing "Shrewsbury has more private cars standing in the streets or running about them than any other town in the country". and Judge Walter Samuel remarked at about the same time "As far as cars on the road are concerned Shrewsbury seems to be outside the ambit of the war completely".

There was unselfishness too. however. Servicemen going on leave who found themselves stranded at Shrewsbury station might well find themselves rescued by one of about a hundred Good Samaritans who at their own expense would get the men home. even as far as the Welsh coast.

Another 'however' – car owners were still in the minority. and fewer still had vehicles actually on the road. The rest were at the mercy of public transport. that is the buses – which made the Midland Red a prime target for attack.

At times it almost seemed as if the Midland Red were a scapegoat on which the totality of public frustration and dissatisfaction could be vented. The services were insufficient. the drivers left before the proper time. they left after the proper time. they didn't leave at all. fares were too high. "Laxities and delays should not be tolerated" – thus the tone of one typical complaint. The strain that resulted from running a service with inadequate resources and insufficient manpower was little appreciated by those who used it.

The bus company was not slow to hit back. Their customers were by no means blameless. they asserted. "Ladies! Ladies!! Ladies!!!" shrieked the adverts. "Some of you are not playing the game. We have repeatedly asked you not to travel on the buses during peak hours. Do not let us ask in vain!!" Soon after they had threatened to issue priority armlets to munition workers. their copy writer once more sharpened his pencil:

> "Prove you are British.
> I will not ride
> Whate'er betide
> During peak hours
> Because I know
> By doing so
> I shall give help
> To the Axis Powers.
> I know this metre
> Is not just right

> But I know quite well
> If you decide tonight
> To lend a hand
> And help the fight
> Our munition lads
> Will make the stuff
> Which will very soon
> Call Adolf's bluff".

Within six months (in July 1941) he had returned to plead. more prosaically. "Ladies and gentlemen. girls and boys. please be wise and sensible and do not wait until the last bus". For all the effect it had it seems doubtful whether anyone read a word of it.

3.—The Regulation of Traffic (Formation of Queues) Order, 1942.

This Order made by the Minister of War Transport on the 16th March, 1942, came into operation on the 12th April, 1942, and provides: —

" Where at any stopping-place (including a stand or terminus) on a tramcar, trolley vehicle or public service vehicle route on any highway provision is made, by means of a barrier rail, or of two parallel barrier rails, for the formation of a queue or line of persons waiting to enter the vehicle such persons shall form and keep the queue or line in manner following that is to say: —

" The queue or line shall commence against the end of the barrier rail or parallel barrier rails nearest to the stopping place of the vehicle and facing the said stopping place and shall continue alongside the barrier rail, or (in the case of parallel barrier rails) between the barrier rails.

" Where no barrier rail is provided, any six or more persons so waiting as aforesaid shall form and keep a queue or line of not more than two abreast on the footway.

" A person shall not take or endeavour to take any position in a queue or line formed in accordance with the provisions of paragraph 1 or paragraph 2 of this Order otherwise than behind the persons already forming the same, or enter or endeavour to enter the vehicle before any other person desiring to enter the same vehicle who stood in front of him in such queue or line.''

Your Committee acting in collaboration with the Midland Red Omnibus Co., Ltd., have provided suitable notices indicating the position where queues shall form, etc.

Some re-arrangement of certain 'bus services operating from the Square and Barker Street Stations has been necessary.

Your Committee are informed that the queues are operating quite satisfactorily, and desire to record their appreciaition of the manner in which the public have co-operated in carrying out the terms of this Order.

The borough council, too, played its part. The council refused to erect queue barriers at the bus terminus in the Square, and turned down an offer by a London firm to build bus shelters, the cost to be borne by advertisers, not the rate-payers. But perhaps the most bewildering aspect of local travel at that time was the question of bus queues. Analogous with the Sherlock Holmes incident of the dog in the night time, the strange thing about bus queues, from the beginning of the war right up to the Spring of 1942, was that there weren't any! Even though everybody wanted them they simply didn't exist. In practical terms, if you were a prop forward from the rugby club you got on a bus, whereas if you happened to be a frail old lady of ninety years, most probably you didn't. To us today with our vision of the archetypal Britisher waiting phlegmatically in an orderly queue it seems impossible, yet so it was.

1939, 1940, 1941 all passed, and then in April 1942 Barker Street was made the main terminus, and with it came a compulsory order that where six or more passengers were gathered together, so must a queue be formed. At last public, press and bus company had been listened to, and thereafter, although chaos continued to reign, it was at least organised chaos. That the authorities were taking the new regulations seriously was proved when they apprehended one Donald Poole and charged him with breaking a bus queue at the Sentinel on 22nd August 1942. He was found guilty and fined £2 with 19/- costs, with the consequences that attention now came to be fastened on such comparatively trivial problems as children monopolising the buses during holiday times and not surrendering seats to their elders.

But for those who concluded that it was easier to walk, there were still hazards to be faced. Wrote W.R.P., parodying Housman:

> "In summer time up Pride Hill
> My love and I would wend,
> And dodge the perambulators
> And circumvent their trend
> To bump us in the end".

Save, Save, Save!

If at all times to save is prudent, and in war-time patriotic as well, then Salopians during the Second War demonstrated both prudence and patriotism. Yet they did more than save – they gave too, which has to be even more of a disinterested act.

Among usual donations to charity were those given on successive Poppy Days, and in November 1943 relish was added by the sight of United States servicemen with their collecting buckets. Contributions had been sent to the Coventry Distress Fund in December 1940, and later in the war Maddox's endowed a cottage home for a blind person as a memorial to the first member of their staff killed in action. Two of the most significant areas of charitable giving were the Spitfire Fund and the Red Cross, the former being a short-term operation in the autumn of 1940 when £5,000 was raised to buy a Spitfire (yes, almost incredibly that sum bought a whole aeroplane in those days), whereas money for the Red Cross was donated throughout the war period. The latter's final figure exceeded £100,000 – the proceeds of flag days, auctions and penny-a-week funds. In September 1940 Queen Elizabeth gave a doll as a draw prize; early the following year Shrewsbury, New Jersey, sent $1,350; Maddox's donated the proceeds of a fashion show. That methods of raising money were many and various is shown by an article in that same year: "A Shrewsbury firm has a swear box with graduated charges from a penny upwards for BOTHER to 6d for _____. Perhaps I had better not give you the full scale. One member of the staff, an ex-sergeant major, has, I hear, applied for a season ticket".

When it came to saving, of course much larger sums were involved. In November 1939 new national savings certificates and defence bonds were issued; soon to form or belong to a savings group became fashionable, and on the corner of Market Street and Swan Hill a 'thermometer' recorded the figure currently reached. 'All together now! Save to win the war' went the slogan, and the citizens of Shrewsbury proceeded to respond, encouraged by that most patriotic of firms, R. Maddox & Co. In July 1940 an aero engine in their window would have caught the stroller's eye, while the following month the attraction there was the famous George Robey (then living in the town) signing autographs for purchasers of savings certificates. A gimmick it might be called today, but every little helped, so that by early 1943 Shrewsbury had been mentioned on the wireless as having saved a staggering £5 million. By the end of the war that figure had swollen to £9 million.

There were also specific causes. 'War Weapons Week' in November 1940 aimed at raising £320,000 for investment in a destroyer named HMS Shrewsbury. 28th February – 7th March 1942 was designated 'Warships Week' during which a total of £655,522 was achieved, and a pleasant postscript to that event took place on 30th August 1945 when at Shrewsbury castle the Australian High Commissioner was presented with a gift of silver plate for HMS Shropshire, by that time part of the Australian navy. Turning skywards, 'Wings for Victory' had for its goal the production of new Spitfires, the public being invited to buy savings stamps and write messages for Hitler on them, those messages to be stuck on bombs and delivered by the RAF. 'Wings for Victory' was marked by a parade on 27th March 1943 reckoned to be the longest procession ever witnessed in Shrewsbury, and so impressive that it prompted one onlooker to observe "The bright colours and the music and the spring sunshine gilding the scene – all these things roused the fierce patriotism that is latent in all of us". A 'Salute the Soldier' campaign followed a year later, and in May 1945 'Victory Savings Week' when all were implored to 'save as hard as ever to win victory in the Far East and stop inflation at home'.

Another way of saving was to avoid waste, yet somehow it was always the other person doing the wasting. The government chivvied the man in the street. 'Don't listen to the squander bug' they yelled at him, and even empowered the police to enter houses to see if fuel was being wasted. Meanwhile the object of their concern was finding examples in plenty of public spending that was quite unnecessary. At the start of the war he complained about payments to ARP workers who would gladly have done the job for nothing, and about part-time members of the Observer Corps getting 1/3 an hour compared with Special Constables (nothing), servicemen (2/- per day) and old-age pensioners (10/- a week). He objected to ATS being given uniforms in which to do clerical jobs. He grumbled when a street savings group was sent a massive parcel of official literature weighing four pounds. That there were flaws in many of the arguments did not prevent those arguments from being vigorously pursued.

Nevertheless, even while beams were being discovered in other people's eyes Shrewsbury went enthusiastically about its business of collecting salvage, voluntarily at first, then from June 1940 as a compulsory exercise. All manner of objects were amassed. During 1940's dark days aluminium saucepans were in demand. Meanwhile the WVS gathered in all the wool it could find and enlisted an army of knitters. The Ministry of Supply appealed for 125,000 pairs of binoculars, donors to take them to the nearest optician. August 1940 found children at Oxon collecting two tons of scrap, but then, children being natural scavengers they were well to the fore in this sort of enterprise, even if all the treasures they contrived to scrape together did not perhaps find their way to the salvage depot at Monkmoor. But let nobody reproach the youngsters specifically. A doll which had been put out for salvage was later seen adorning the radiator of a refuse collection lorry.

From March 1942, to waste paper became a punishable offence, and throughout the war, books were particularly valuable salvage. Someone calculated that one book per household in the borough could provide six million cartridge cases; in fact Shrewsbury did better still, for in 1944 between 4th and 18th March (when a Book Recovery Drive was held) no fewer than 70,000 books were collected. One woman was proud to have saved 5,000 bus tickets (receptacles on the buses were a late innovation), and the mayor, Harry Steward, was moved to compose a ditty on the whole theme:

> "Sing a song of paper
> All colours shape and size,
> Nine and ninety lorry loads
> May win for us the prize.
> If all the folk in Shrewsbury
> Will do what they are bid,
> The Royal Salop Infirmary
> Will get 250 quid".

PAPER AND CARDBOARD

Paper and cardboard and cartons provide
food containers for the troops; rifle cases,
cases for shells. One old envelope will
make a cartridge wad.

HOUSEHOLD BONES

Household bones are turned into glue for
aeroplanes, etc., glycerine for explosives,
fertiliser, feeding stuffs. If every household
gave 2 oz. a week the country would get
over 20,000 tons of bones a year.

METALS, TINS

Metals, including tins, will give the country
aeroplanes, tanks, guns. One ton of metal
makes 150 shell cases for 18-pdr. shells.

RAGS, OLD CLOTHING

Rags, old clothing, stockings, etc., provide
rugs, blankets, uniforms. Clean woollen
waste, when graded, is valuable.

FOOD SCRAPS

Food scraps are used to feed pigs and
poultry. 1,000 houses provide one ton of
edible kitchen waste per week. One ton
of kitchen waste per week will feed 40 pigs.

Yet the war was approaching its last days when Shrewsbury's most memorable salvage operation was conceived. The London borough of Hackney, having suffered more than most from the enemy's rocket raids, was adopted by the WVS of Shrewsbury and the surrounding area, and a collection of household articles organised. In March 1945 the first consignment of furniture and other effects was ready. The mayor helped to load it, and away it went along the A5 to London. A further twenty-five lorry loads were promised, and by May a total of two hundred tons had been sent. The gratitude of the people of Hackney knew no bounds. A Shrewsbury reporter who visited the area found himself treated like a hero. He was moved to see women weeping with joy: an unashamedly sentimental occasion that proved blessed to giver and receiver alike.

Workers' playtime

There was rationing of this and there was rationing of that; shortages here, gaps on the shelves there. One commodity, however, that war-time Shrewsbury did not go short of was entertainment. While the war pared down certain leisure activities, others it seemed to stimulate.

This was the great era of cinema going. Where the town now has one cinema it then had four, playing to full houses; films many of whose titles (because of television) are still familiar to a different generation today. Long queues were common: to see Chaplin's 'The Great Dictator', or 'Mrs. Miniver', or 'Random Harvest' for example. There were also films now long since forgotten such as the 'The Nine Men of the Eighth Army.' In the early days of the war controversy raged as to whether cinemas should open on Sundays. Yes, said the council, the police, the Anglicans and the R.C.'s. No, replied the Free Churches, while Councillor T. G. Robin declared that it would be a menace to the home life of the borough. It took a year to settle the argument. Even then it was only the Granada at first that was allowed to open its doors – and then not until 7.45 p.m. Another twelve months were to pass before 5 p.m. Sunday screenings were permitted.

Cinemas, so popular then, are still with us. What has passed into oblivion is the concert party – revue type of entertainment which abounded forty years ago. Their names were legion: Salopia Follies, Happy Days Variety Company, the KSLI Super-optimists, the Queries (ATS), Att-a-girl, and most prominent of all in those days, the RAPCATS (as the Royal Army Pay Corps and the ATS girls called themselves). They gave so many excellent shows locally (they even broadcast on one occasion in October 1940) that the Shrewsbury Chronicle was moved to write "As for entertaining the troops, the troops are entertaining us".

Receivers were eagerly tuned in for the 'Workers' Playtime' broadcast from the Sentinel on 7th April 1942. Also that year there were Sunday variety concerts at the Empire, circuses visited the town regularly, while a pantomime 'Sleeping Beauty' at the Granada in January 1944 generated a five-hour queue for tickets. Business was indeed booming, and from the boom sprang a local comedian, Aubrey Lucas, who achieved more than local fame by appearing on radio's 'Variety Bandbox' at the end of the war.

'Variety Bandbox' had its resident comedian, and so did Shrewsbury with the legendary George Robey (then in his seventies) living near the Column. Many other famous light entertainers visited the town. Joyce Grenfell in September 1941, Harry Parr-Davies (pianist and composer of so many of Gracie Fields' songs), Stainless Stephen, Anona Winn and Margaret Eaves appeared at the Empire. To the Granada came Cyril Fletcher, Forsyth Seaman and Farrell, Frederick Ferrari, Charlie Chester, Elsie and Doris Waters. Perhaps it was all too much; maybe it was satiety which prompted a critic to remark of pianists Rawicz and Landauer "No doubt some of the audience would have appreciated an admixture of more solid fare". Harry Parry and his Swing Sextet were other musicians who appeared, so that one is tempted to claim that the Granada forty years ago catered for a wider public than it does today, with bingo now the only diet on offer.

Eager dancers squeezed into Lewis's dance hall in Castlefields; and at Morris's, Pride Hill, the 260 maximum was seldom adhered to. 2/6 rising to 3/- was the going rate for a dance, although when Jan Berenska and his Radio Rhythm Five, with Lieutenant Eddie Carroll at the piano, played at Morris's on 14th April 1944 the cost soared to 5/-. But that was an evening dress function. Dances would start at 6.30 and finish at 10 p.m. – until March 1941 when an extra hour was granted. Spot prizes might inlude an onion, an egg or a sausage, thereby adding greatly to the romantic atmosphere of the evening.

There was one area of need – the theatre. Of drama groups in the town, pride of place was occupied by the Croft Hermits, a hard-working and talented society who joined ENSA and who in the first three years after the war started gave 136 performances – for part-timers a phenomenal number. But Shrewsbury could have done with a professional repertory company, and the occasional appearance at the army's garrison theatre of such well-known stage personalities as Barry K. Barnes, Diana Churchill and Emlyn Williams was small compensation for its lack.

How did the outbreak of war in September 1939 affect the sporting scene? The nation had scarcely had time to try on its gas-masks before a lady was offering the War Office the loan of her beagles "for the purpose of providing recreation and out-of-door exercise for officers convalescent after wounds received on active service", in response to which a suitably grateful War Office promised to take the animals 'on strength' in due course. Only a little slower was the fox-hunting set, one of whom asserted "We owe a very certain duty to our men at the front to carry on hunting till this war is over".

But these were the rarefied heights. Ordinary people too had their sporting pleasures, despite the fact that, unlike fox-hunting, other pursuits could not always be guaranteed freedom from interruption. Racing flourished, many war-time meetings being held on the old Meole course; four thousand attended on Whit Monday 1943, and the August meeting that year included American trotting horse races in sulkies. Meanwhile, cyclists pedalled on, skaters took advantage in January 1940 of a Severn frozen from Greyfriars to Port Hill, Pengwern Boat Club oarsmen rowed as and when they could, if not competitively.

On 12th August the army Infantry Training Corps played cricket against North Wales on the Shrewsbury School ground. The event is notable in that it was about the only cricket match of any consequence that took place in Shrewsbury during the whole six years of war. George Hart, ex-Middlesex, later coach at the Schools, played and so did Emrys Davies (Glamorgan) and R. Sale (Warwickshire); the poor attendance at the game may denote the low ebb to which cricket had sunk. At village and club level it had almost disappeared from sight, with many doubting whether it could ever be revived, and its virtual demise, almost alone among ball games, remains one of the time's minor mysteries.

Tennis and golf suffered much less drastically; indeed able-bodied young men found themselves condemned for taking part in both these games. The golf club's answer was to invite Flight Lieutenant Henry Cotton to play an exhibition match, while in the cause of tennis the Woodfield club defended the right of the war worker to relax on the court, and donated the proceeds of a tournament to the Red Cross. That competitive table tennis continued to be played. Mayor Harry Steward could have testified, for he was both active in the game and proficient at it.

Yet it seems fitting that the game seemingly least affected by the furies of war should be that most English and, to the observer, that most gentle of games – bowls. Bowls continued on its traditional and unobtrusive way, apparently with scarcely a thought for the wider scene, so that one gentleman was constrained to remark "If we had a parachute invasion our local bowlers would see what could be done about fixing up a match with the Dusseldorf and District League". A nice touch.

So from the homespun to the more exotic. It may be that on 10th October 1942 some of those bowlers whose season had recently ended were among those making their expectant way to Gay Meadow to witness, not a football match but – baseball. The Flying Eagles beat the Yankee All Stars that day, with such colourful characters on view as Dead Eye Delaney, Walloping Wood, Slinking Hank and Snooty Schneider: reproducing an occasion twenty-four years earlier when towards the end of the First War, Canadians and United States players had battled it out on the same pitch.

Having reached the Gay Meadow we shall halt a while. Football in Shrewsbury during World War Two was in a curious state, charged with frustrations yet bringing its excitements too. The frustrations were caused by the manner in which Shrewsbury Town FC was anaesthetised for the duration. The club played no games at all in seasons 1940–41 and 1941–42, and thereafter only occasionally, until the end of the war when they applied unsuccessfully to join Division Three of the Football League. Local amateur soccer likewise slumbered until August 1942 at which date its league was re-formed.

September 1939 had seen 'the Town' about to enjoy its third season in the Midland League. Instead a series of attractive friendly matches was arranged against such famous clubs as Coventry, West Bromwich, Birmingham City, Preston, and Manchester United. Blackpool were beaten 5-0, while scores of 6-4 against Cardiff City and 4-7 at home to Nottingham Forest suggest open games that would have gladdened eager war-time crowds. Yet soon after that the club had virtually ceased to exist.

Four thousand watched the Shropshire Cup Final between Wellington and the RAF in April 1941, and when the same teams clashed again a year later, on view were two famous players – O'Donnell of Blackpool and Burbanks of Sunderland. Six months earlier the Shrewsbury Chronicle's 'Guvnor' had seen Wolves play Cardiff and had remarked on "a Shropshire lad with a mop of fair hair – the star of the game". It was not the last sporting occasion on which Billy Wright was to be the star.

As a spectator sport, war-time football in Shrewsbury was saved by the likes of Billy Wright – stars of the future, present and past, who through being stationed in the area were able to grace Gay Meadow with their skills in representative games. Finch and Richardson of the Albion, Hancocks (later Wright's colleague at Wolverhampton), Doherty the Irish international, Mountford (Stoke) and Bray of Manchester City all made appearances. On 12th February 1944 included in an RAF side was one L.A.C.

Revie. At Easter that year six thousand saw a Shropshire Sportsmen's Eleven beat Wrexham 6-0, and the contest between Tommy Lawton, centre-forward for Wrexham, and Frank Swift in the opposing goal would have been a fascinating one. Tommy having failed to score made up for it the following Christmas when the result read RAF 3 Sportsmen's Eleven 14. The half-time score was 1-8. That rare scorer Stanley Matthews got one, Lawton six. High individual scoring was not infrequent in those days, for early in Shrewsbury Town's first season after the war we find Richardson (ex-Albion) grabbing all the goals in the 7-0 win over Notts County.

That bank holidays and longer summer breaks should be subject to war-time constraints was inevitable, yet generally people contrived to make the best of them. Carnivals, local shows, fetes all tended to disappear during the first half of the war and resurrect themselves from about 1943 onwards, but the two principal outdoor events in the Shrewsbury calendar – the West Midlands Show in May and the Flower Show three months later – were not held again until 1947.

Where did people go on their days out? Boating on the river was always popular. So were bathing at Shelton Roughs and walking on Haughmond Hill, and it is a sign how times have changed that on a fine summer's day in the 1980s it is quite possible to visit both these spots and find them otherwise deserted. Listening to the bands in the Quarry was a favourite pastime also, and many top military bands were in attendance, especially in the early years of the war – the Coldstream, Royal Horse and Welsh Guards, and the Royal Marines.

The Midland Red advertised trips to Aberystwyth (9/-) and Chester (4/6) at Easter 1940. Whit Bank Holiday that year was cancelled, the August one virtually a non-event, and it was not until Easter Monday 1941 that the first authorised break in war production came. On August Monday that year government appeals not to travel were widely disregarded, and because of that it was thought an end to bank holidays might well have come. However, 1942 brought a reversal. The grim nature of war news and the increased bite of petrol rationing put an end to pleasure motoring for the vast majority, and from then until the end of the war local amusements such as sports and fetes became synonymous with the bank holiday scene.

And the week's break from the factory, shop or office each July or August? 'Drop work and worries' one advert insisted. 'Push the war into the background of your mind. Come to this resort of youth and gaiety'. Times must indeed have changed, for this, it seems, was New Brighton, 1940 style. Some obeyed the injunction of course, but many more did not and as the war went on it began to be thought that Shrewsbury should be doing something to cater for the patriotic, stay-at-home holiday-maker. The idea caught on and in 1942 a 'Holidays at Home' project was conceived, a sort of domestic wakes fortnight. That Rotary and not the borough council did the organising probably accounted for its success, for success it was. An extensive sports programme was arranged: angling contests, boxing tournaments, open-air whist. There were river picnics and talent spotting competitions in the Quarry. "Shrewsbury has not had such a gay time for years" enthused the Chronicle, and indeed the programme seems to have been imaginatively planned, even allowing that not everyone would have found an evening tour of the borough allotments totally absorbing. Although most events were free, no less than £554 was collected for the Red

Cross and the Infirmary, a result which persuaded the corporation that it would do well to step in and organise a similar scheme in 1943. It did; the effect (to widespread public disgust) being that 'Holidays at Home' that year comprised merely an extended series of band concerts! "The council does not care two hoots about the workers, or servicemen and women who are doing their job for the national effort" fulminated a Yorkshire correspondent to the Chronicle, which prompted the reply "If Yorkshireman does not like Shrewsbury let him return to Ilkley Moor or keep indoors and refrain from comment". As a rational counter-argument it seemed to lack a certain intellectual weight.

Finally, the performing arts. Shrewsbury was not well served for theatre, as we have seen. As for the ballet, that would scarcely have been heard of. Music, however, tells a different story, and here credit must devolve on F. C. Morris, conductor for twenty-one years of the Shrewsbury Orchestral Society, which orchestra regularly gave performances in the Alington Hall at Shrewsbury School and at the Technical College. A slighting remark made at the time to the effect that Shrewsbury audiences wanted to hear hackneyed works only, is not borne out by the programmes actually presented to them. A typical concert on 16th March 1945 consisted of Borodin's 1st symphony and the Sibelius Violin Concerto, while three months earlier Brahms' Song of Destiny had been performed with the local choral society. Other programmes had included Brahms' B Flat Piano Concerto, Bach's in D Minor, and the Mozart K488, with soloists as renowned as Myra Hess, Eileen Joyce and Louis Kentner. Indeed there was hardly a distinguished pianist in the country who did not play in Shrewsbury at some time during the war, for besides those already named Pouishnoff, Clifford Curzon, Cyril Smith, Phyllis Sellick, Moiseiwitsch and Kathleen Long all came, also violinists Arthur Catterall, Jelly d'Aranyi, Ida Haendel, Alfred Cave and Albert Sandler. Similarly in the case of singers: Parry Jones sang Elgar's little-performed 'King Olaf', Isobel Baillie, Elsie Suddaby, Astra Desmond and Jan van der Gucht all sang in St. Chad's Church, and other notable guests were Olive Groves, Dennis Noble, Roy Henderson and Richard Tauber. A musical roll of honour indeed.

Strange to learn that the performance of 'Messiah' on 19th December 1940 was the first in the town for twenty years; slightly incongruous that appearing in a popular concert at the Empire in November 1943 was Sergeant Edmund Rubbra. The musical event of those war years? Perhaps the visit of John Barbirolli and the Halle Orchestra on 24th, 25th and 26th January 1944. Barbirolli professed himself charmed with Shrewsbury and its lovely audiences; moreover the Severn reminded him of his beloved Elgar. He gave every penny of his fee to the Red Cross: a warm-hearted man as well as a conductor of genius.

Middle-aged town

Youngsters in the 1980s might be surprised to learn the extent to which juvenile crime was being committed during the period 1939–45, and if thus surprised might this be because it is customary for each rising generation to be told how much worse it is than the one that has gone before?

In July 1940 an increase in teenage crime was reported. The following month that increase had become "alarming": a 41% rise during the first year of the war. By 1941 the figure had again swollen, and so it continued. The details are all too familiar: vandalism at Cock's Tannery, garage breaking, shop breaking, wrecked gardens at Harlescott, plants, hedges, fences destroyed, bulbs stolen from the Quarry. Causes, as usual, were not hard to find. A generation earlier it had been penny dreadfuls, now in 1941 it was gangster films (television's turn was yet to come). And of course there was education, which was simply not delivering the goods.

Even if families were not being broken up by legal separation and divorce, the absence of fathers away in the forces could have a similarly deleterious effect. Because so many children were sleepy in the mornings it was seriously suggested that schools might delay their start until 9.30 a.m., and indeed much truancy was caused by families getting up late and children subsequently not bothering to go to school. Manners also came in for admonition. "Everyone can see that the general behaviour of too large a section of present day children has deteriorated" wrote a correspondent to the Chronicle, and earlier there had been complaints about their travelling in over-crowded buses. Couldn't they walk? Why were children so lazy nowadays?

Under-age drinking was also a problem. A fifteen-year old girl drinker had a 10.30 p.m. curfew imposed and was bound over for six months, while three sixteen-year olds who drank in the 'Slipper' were told in court "You have not only disgraced yourselves but also your family and friends".

Were the penalties meted out inadequate? Were no effective deterrents available? "Methods of punishment are largely ineffective" admitted the leader writer of the Shrewsbury Chronicle, and this is strange, for were not those methods the very ones so often being called for to combat today's teenage crime? The courts had no hesitation then in ordering the birch; in June 1940 a boy who stole 5/- (and returned 2/7 of it) was beaten. Lads as young as nine were given six strokes for breaking and entering. An older man convicted of assault had to endure twelve strokes of the birch as well as being sent to prison. A young woman who abandoned her baby ("I was unable to find a home for it") was sentenced to two months hard labour. How much harsher would punitive measures need to be in order to deter, and by the time that point was reached, would legitimate punishment have degenerated into savagery?

Hand in hand with public disquiet about the youth of the borough went (as is normal) dissatisfaction with the state of education, but it was not on the whole a dissatisfaction which the radical Education Act of 1944 was to do very much to dispel. That act came into force as a result of a conviction in enlightened circles that educational opportunity ought to be more widely spread; where hitherto only a small minority had attended anything but an elementary school, the new bill sought to provide secondary education for all. In July 1943 the government published its white paper on Educational Reconstruction, and a bill followed it five months later which swiftly became law. Few qualms were expressed at the time about the grammar-secondary modern dichotomy, although speaking in Shrewsbury in 1941 Chuter Ede, who was parliamentary secretary to the Board of Education, had declared himself against selection. Raising of the school leaving age to fifteen (which had been due in September 1939 but then suspended) was postponed until April 1947, and an amendment to the bill to raise the age to sixteen was defeated only narrowly.

Among most elementary teachers the new act was seen as providing an opportunity for children to develop according to their abilities and inclinations. Shrewsbury's senior councillor, T. G. Robin, ex-headmaster of the Lancasterian School, called it "a triumph of the spirit of the country – a system of education that would benefit every child". A less idealistic view was canvassed among many influential citizens: that it would add fifty per cent to the rates bill.

Prior to the act, gloomy views about education had been of two distinct sorts. The first, and probably less firmly expressed, view was of working-class children suffering disadvantage: who, because the school certificate was denied them, were without access to a wide range of jobs for which many of them would have been well suited. "Mixing with men in the army" wrote the Chronicle's 'Guvnor', looking back to an earlier war, "I was impressed with the general inadequacy of their schooling". Since then, had very much changed?

An opposite, and rather more sonorous, opinion harked back to a past golden age (which usually coincided with the commentator's own youth) when a spirit of good sense and rightness prevailed. This view was typified by a correspondent from Oakengates in February 1943 who expressed it thus: "In the old days the three Rs were the foundation of all teaching, and I think the children were much better educated then than now". The years have passed but the same sentiments are still being expressed today.

To holders of the second view, anything in the nature of an educational frill was anathema. During World War Two, head teachers in Shropshire schools were allowed clerical help for the first time, and this provoked a storm. Alderman Mrs. E. M. Cock staunchly defended the innovation, but the Chronicle attacked it and so did many of the public, one of whom wrote in June 1941 "If this country had spent less on fancy educational fads in the last twenty years and more on warships, tanks and aircraft we should be in a much better position today". Two other proposed measures attracted violent opposition. When the Education Committee suggested early in 1943 that a psychologist be appointed in the interests of retarded children, the Reverend R. A. Giles thought that the former's first job should be to interview the committee members who had voted for him in the first place. Later the reverend gentleman spoke more strongly still. "I refuse to believe" he said "that Shropshire children are built like that. If it is so it is time this country went into a definite policy of sterilization". The Chronicle called the proposed appointment "the quack remedy", which two corres-pondents – the vicar of Cressage and the Reverend G. Kendal Dovey, Prestfelde School's headmaster (the latter of whom also opposed birching) – were quick to refute. The other point of controversy arose from the committee's wish to employ a drama organiser for the area, "a post of such doubtful necessity" as the Chronicle called it, and provoking one Civis to write that, although liking plays and music "I no more wish to see these recreations on the rates than I would wish to see a whisky and soda or a football match paid for from the same source". Again it was a point of view that commanded widespread support. "They have no mandate whatever to adopt a policy of reckless spending" said the Chronicle. That paper was talking about a proposal to open branch libraries in the borough, but the principle seemed roughly the same.

There is evidence that then, even more than now, the young saw Shrewsbury as not only a 'Middle Ages' town but a middle-aged one as well, for not even their having joined the forces exempted them from being pursued by complaints. Sometimes the complaints were oblique as in the case of grumbles about the noise of aircraft over the town; sometimes more direct. "During a recent visit to the Records Office I observed that one girl was more occupied in improving and keeping up her facial beauty than on work" was one such. Another concerned the unseemly conduct of officers and their lady friends. "A woman accompanying an officer should help him to keep his dignity by being a lady and dressing accordingly. Hats, for instance, are an essential for good taste". Or this complaint, during a hot spell in the summer of 1942, of "the number of young men and women whom one meets nowadays sun worshipping for sun tan with complete disregard for soul purification". Particularly repugnant seem the objections raised by local residents when Doctor Barnado's Children's Home proposed moving to The Mount.

After a Mr. Belton of the Chamber of Commerce had written in disapproval of contemporary youth, one serving officer replied (in November 1940) "There can be few towns in England or elsewhere which offer less opportunity to the younger generation to satisfy their ambitions or are more adept at squashing their ardour . . . over everything the hand of the middle-aged squeezes tightly with an unimaginative, class-conscious and smug grip". But to be fair to Mr. Belton, perhaps it lies within the nature of things for the old to be jealous of the young, and perhaps that is why, when the morals of the young were called into question it was sexual morality that loomed largest in their critics' minds.

But of course morality meant something more than that. About the time that the war was entering its middle phase, whispers of certain ideas to reshape the social life of Britain began to be heard. Those ideas were to find expression in the Beveridge Plan. Beveridge himself was not a young man, yet perhaps the young saw him as a formulator of young ideas, and his plan as an attempt to create a world more to their liking and nearer to their ideal. Not all saw it thus. The Beveridge Report was opposed, usually not openly but more subtly. The worker didn't want to be coddled. There were references to the dead hand of the state and the smothering burden of bureaucracy. The word 'freedom' was much bandied about. But in Shrewsbury in 1939 we find the mayor appealing on behalf of needy children, and a Boot Fund still in operation, and it was the young who disliked the idea of paternalistic charity more than the middle-aged and the old.

However, in the end, in July 1945, over the country as a whole if not in Shrewsbury itself, it was the turn of the young to have their way.

"Forward – by the right"

Party politics during the Second War fell into two phases. Initially, and then during the dark days of 1940, 1941 and 1942 with more urgent matters requiring attention, they were pushed into the background. However, once the corner had been turned, the party die-hards could hardly wait to get their hands round one another's throats.

While it suited the Conservatives to fly the flag of unity, to the opposition parties patriotic gestures of that nature were of little help. Local government elections were suspended for the duration immediately war was declared, an arrangement which accommodated the sitting members to perfection. Henceforth vacancies were filled through nomination and selection, and not surprisingly much ill-feeling was generated. Controversies arose, for example at Meole Brace when a new councillor was selected in private, and in Ditherington a 300-name petition in favour of a certain candidate was ignored by the men in power. Shrewsbury's council resembled an exclusive club, and an ageing one at that, for of the forty-one members in 1943 thirty-one would not see sixty again.

More than one rate-payer looked forward to electing a younger, more representative council after the war, yet one man there was who on 9th November 1945 had completed a seven-year spell in office with scarcely a word being said against him in that time. Local grocer Harry Steward had been Shrewsbury's mayor for ten months when the war came, and its mayor he remained until after hostilities were over. Safe to say that the borough has never had a more popular first citizen. The Chronicle referred to his "breezy humour and homeliness of manner" and commented "It is a further insight to see him at work in his little office off Pride Hill, with his cat, and the presents sent to him by former boy scouts now overseas" – an affectionate and memorable portrait.

Well-known politicians who visited Shrewsbury at this time included Harold Nicolson, Parliamentary Secretary to the Minister of Information, Margaret Bondfield from the Home Office (who in 1924 had been Britain's first woman cabinet minister), R. S. Hudson (Minister of Agriculture), and Lord Woolton (Food): all members of Churchill's National Government, Churchill having succeeded the unfortunate Neville Chamberlain after the German invasion of the Low Countries in May 1940. Support for the new Prime Minister, in Parliament and in the country, was widespread – to the satisfaction of Shrewsbury's Tory MP, Lieutenant Arthur Duckworth. Duckworth had previously accused the Labour and Liberal parties of breaking the political truce by insinuating party politics into national affairs; truth to tell, a song whose notes were to be heard increasingly as the war progressed.

But for the time being patriotism was popular. Later the dilemma was to become more apparent: whether to accept the government's conduct of the war unquestioningly, or criticise incompetence when it became manifest; a dilemma which evoked some sympathy when the critic was known to be on the right of the political spectrum but which otherwise was regarded as faintly treacherous. However, during the first six months of 1942 (the nadir of the Allied cause) censure became almost respectable. so total were the disasters. January that year saw the Government under attack in the Commons. In February Churchill was criticised for an evasive speech: some even wanted to send for Lloyd George! The Shrewsbury Chronicle. who in May was protesting "Many of us have our own views on the conduct of the war but this is no time to air them" had. within the month. after the heavy defeat in Libya. reacted somewhat differently: "The general feeling is that serious blunders have been made".

Alamein and the subsequent clearing of North Africa meant that thoughts could first lightly brush against. then as time passed. touch more firmly upon. the post-war scene: and it seems ironic in view of later developments that the Labour party should be generally optimistic about post-war conditions while Conservatives should be forecasting a long period of austerity. Late in 1943 the first faint whispers of a general election might be heard. a more welcome sound to the Socialists than to their opponents. Rumours arose of the formation of a new centre party (which proved premature by a matter of decades). and then in November 1944 an election to follow the end of the war in Europe was announced. The Chronicle feared the immediate demise of national unity. Moreover there would. it declared. be little to fight about: personalities would decide the issue – an assessment which proved to be very wrong indeed.

What sort of state were the political parties in as a result of government by coalition? Locally and nationally. partly because Churchill as a leader was supposed to be above party. the Conservatives had sunk into inertia until in September 1943 they roused themselves sufficiently to issue a battle cry 'Forward – by the right'. and (in order to keep Labour at bay) advocate a continuation of the coalition after the war. Would Shrewsbury MP. Arthur Duckworth. be re-selected as candidate? This was far from certain. for Duckworth had attracted some controversy and was not popular in every quarter. Nevertheless he was asked to stand and accepted.

Perhaps the Tories' strongest card was the public detestation of bureaucracy. an evil widely identified with Socialism. The Labour party would seek to curtail the power of Parliament and increase that of the executive – so the story ran. But any measure of surprise that accompanied the Labour victory of 1945 was newly-found. for earlier in the war such a win had generally been expected. Faced with the formidable task of contesting the Shrewsbury seat for Labour was Flight Lieutenant Stanley Chapman MBE. a Londoner who had been adopted as candidate as long ago as 1939.

As for the Liberals. quietly operating under the umbrella of the Beveridge Plan. their candidate was to be the well-known KC. A. S. Comyns Carr. whose platform included (needless to say?) rating reform and proportional representation.

And the fourth party? The Shrewsbury Communist Party had its headquarters at Talbot Chambers in Market Street. and 1941–43 were its halcyon years. coinciding with that great wave of pro-Soviet feeling which resulted from Russia's defiance of the Nazi invader. Public meetings. delegations in favour of a Second Front. fund-raising on behalf of Russian horses. lectures by Professor J. B. Haldane. William Rust (editor of the Daily Worker). and Dean Hewlett Johnson of Canterbury (the Red Dean): then suddenly. with the Western allies establishing themselves in Europe. and Russia's popularity on the wane, it was all over, a phenomenon as quick in growth and decline as a jungle flower.

Nobody under the age of twenty-nine had ever voted in a general election before, one unpredictable factor among many. "I rather fancy that you will find it difficult to make up your minds which way to vote" rather condescendingly wrote the Shrewsbury Chronicle's 'Guvnor' in an open letter to the forces, while that newspaper's leader writer, commenting on the friendly spirit among the parties, counselled "Let us while differing remain friends". That was Christmas 1944, and what signs of goodwill there were then did not long survive it. As 1945 dawned so did the politicians deliver thrust and counter-thrust. The Conservatives were a not a class party, declared Duckworth; a wide distribution of private property was the surest foundation of a stable society. Comyns Carr's opinion was that Churchill should not have accepted the Tory leadership. "No one who supported Mr. Chamberlain should be elected to the next Parliament" he affirmed, and "Private enterprise must not be allowed to fleece the public". Labour accused the Tories of destroying the League of Nations. When Stanley Chapman announced "We planned for war, now we must plan for peace", the Chronicle urged its readers to beware of catch phrases and reminded them that full employment would mean direction of labour.

In February circumstances dealt the local Conservatives a body blow. Duckworth's divorce was made public. The news came as something of an embarrassment to his party, and in March an all-party debate in the Belmont Hall had to take place without Tory representation. The following month it was announced that Duckworth would not be standing after all – for business reasons, it was hinted; and a successor had to be chosen. "He should be a fairly young man" advised the Chronicle "with the prospect of a long parliamentary life". The advice did not go unheeded! Lieutenant Commander John Langford Holt was only twenty-nine, an ideal candidate who confirmed his suitability in a reassuringly orthodox adoption speech. Controls must be removed immediately peace came. Britain's strength lay in her empire. Like Theodore Roosevelt, we must talk peace but carry a big stick.

Meanwhile the sniping continued. "Let's get rid of the old gang in Shrewsbury. It's time someone else had a go". Thus a Labour supporter, accusing the Tories of having reduced Britain to a state of unpreparedness for war. "Politically Labour appears to me to have no morals" opined that well-known local composer and general practitioner Doctor A. E. Nicholls. A week before VE Day a by-election at Chelmsford resulted in a government defeat, and because, with the war in Europe over, the Socialists would not accede to Churchill's request for the coalition to be kept until victory over Japan had been secured, the Prime Minister formally resigned on 23rd May and then continued at the head of a caretaker administration. The Tories' confidence was scarcely dented. To them, Clement Attlee remained an uninspiring figure whom few were likely to want as a war leader.

Polling day was fixed for Thursday 5th July. The opposition would have preferred a later date in order to maximise the service vote, although in the event it probably made little difference. Because of the far-flung nature of so many of the electorate three weeks would elapse before the result was known. June saw many political meetings in Shrewsbury's streets. When Holt (standing as a 'National' Conservative) was questioned about housing he promised to do his best, for he said he had not found a house for himself yet! ('Labour elected means houses erected' ran the opposition slogan, but whether they would have erected one for Holt is another matter). Much was made in Conservative circles of the Socialist scare, for example that a Labour government would appropriate savings and recruit secret police, that power would come to be invested in the party caucus not Parliament; besides which, of local advantage was Holt's status as a Shrewsbury man. Mr. L. Gillis of Old Coleham denied it forcibly. A Salopian for Shrewsbury? What had Shrewsbury seen of Holt? "Only his small upper class associates know him intimately". Who it was that about this time slashed the Conservative agent's tyres was never discovered.

Comyns Carr, a slightly old-fashioned figure in his high wing-collar, might well have been hampered in his campaign by the attitude of his party leader, Archibald Sinclair, who was not enthusiastic about the election. Certainly neither Comyns Carr nor Chapman was helped by the Chronicle, for whom Churchill was the man. Was this the time to take a risk?, was very much the Chronicle's theme.

The weather for polling day was better than certain of the arrangements for polling had been. Some voters found themselves disenfranchised. Declared 'The Guvnor': "They should have compiled the voting list not from national registration cards but income tax records because they miss nobody". Also incensed were the schoolchildren from St. Giles: theirs was the only primary school not used for voting!

On 26th July the result was declared outside the Technical College: Holt 15,174, Chapman 10,580, Comyns Carr 8,142. Like much else, the national swing had passed Shrewsbury by. Elsewhere Harold Macmillan, Brendan Bracken, James Grigg, Hore Belisha, L. S. Amery, Duncan Sandys (all members of the government) lost their seats. Also beaten were Lady Violet Bonham Carter, William Beveridge and Richard Acland. "We made the grave mistake of starting the mud slinging" admitted Ludlow's Tory MP.

The contrast between the destinies of winner and losers is startling. Comyns Carr and Chapman were irretrievably sunk while Holt was to cling tenaciously to his Shrewsbury seat for the best part of forty years.

"When are you going back?"

July 1939 ... in those early days we looked on them as heroes. "Guests of the nation" we called them, Hore Belisha's young militiamen, one hundred and fifty of whom were soon reporting to Copthorne Barracks from around Shrewsbury ... Hereford ... Birmingham. Secrecy had been deemed unnecessary then, but by the time the next contingent was called we were at war and "somewhere in Shropshire" was the only information as to its destination that it was considered safe for us to have. Meanwhile the 10th Shrewsbury Company of ATS had been formed at 2 Claremont Buildings, and with the Reserves being called up, the great recruiting machine was slipping inexorably into high gear.

As carnivorous a machine as Madame Guillotine a century and a half earlier, it was housed locally at the old Wyle Cop Schools, where on 30th March 1940 the Princess Royal (revisiting Shrewsbury after seven years) was witness to its efficiency and energy. Another who can testify to its voracity is Mr. Alan Morgan, who on Thursday 1st August 1940, as a callow eighteen-year old seeking to make a tentative enquiry, approached its doors to find (ostensibly most reassuring of symbols) a Royal Air Force flight sergeant dozing in the sun. "I ... I want to join the Air Force" stammered young Morgan. "Please" he added, for he had been nicely brought up. His nervousness was not helped by his getting the directions wrong, blundering through the wrong door and being confronted by a sergeant (a gentleman from Hadley named Roberts, whom he knew) in the wrong coloured uniform. However, the situation was quickly put right, for no sooner had our young hopeful found the appropriate department than he had been examined by five doctors, interviewed, accepted and instructed to report to RAF Blackpool the following Monday. Next please.

With so many Army and Air Force units in the vicinity Shrewsbury became virtually a garrison town, its streets an entanglement of khaki and blue that formed an ever-rich, ever-changing pattern. Troops came and went, there were men on embrocation' leave (as one mother put it), there were children playing commandos instead of cowboys and Indians, there was the tramp of heavy feet. The 6th battalion KSLI went on an endurance march and completed 150 miles in five days. The champion ATS drill platoon gave a display in Barker Street, prompting the comment 'If platoon drill is not much use it can at least be made ornamental". The RAF celebrated its silver jubilee, Lyth Hill served as a cadet camp, the Princess Royal came yet again and inspected the barracks. 'Salute the Soldier' week was attended by an impressive display of military might.

In the earlier stages of the war to be in uniform was considered a fine thing. Firms boasted about how many of their employees had joined up. In the first month Maddox's made known the departure of twenty-seven of their staff. Patriotically-slanted ads. appeared, for example for the Shropshire Tyre Company ("75% of our staff have gone voluntarily to do their bit"), while Ronald Beck was able to announce that he and "every member of my former staff is now in the RAF". A later variation on this theme was conceived by those desirous of complaining or protesting about something, justification being provided by such riders as "five of my seven children are now serving".

Whether or not the complaints were justified, the pride most certainly was, and Shrewsbury's Roll of Honour (of the dead and of the surviving) deserves the compliment of more detailed chronicling than is possible here. General Auchinlech, who became General Officer commanding Middle East Forces, was ex-KSLI; Sir Bernard Paget, deputy CIGS and later C-in-C Middle East, was an ex-Salopian, and so was the flier and writer Richard Hillary. Flying Officer M. L. Hulton-Harrop is believed to have been the war's first local casualty, killed over the east coast on 6th September 1939, while one death mourned throughout the borough was that of the mayor's elder son, Michael Steward, pilot and victim of the Normandy invasion.

Eric Lock Road (Lyth Hill) commemorates the son of a Shrewsbury farmer. By December 1940 Pilot Officer Lock, twenty-one years of age, had been awarded the DSO, and DFC and bar, and credited with having shot down twenty-two enemy aircraft. On leave in May 1941, now a Flight Lieutenant, he received a hero's welcome, being much in demand as guest-of-honour at local functions, a pleasant interlude which in retrospect was to assume poignancy. When, after 'missing' had become 'presumed dead', R. Maddox & Co. published 'The story of a brave Shropshire airman', the first edition was sold out immediately to Eric Lock's proudly honouring townspeople.

On a more mundane level honour was also being paid to all the troops in Shrewsbury by those volunteers who helped to run the various service canteens that sprang up in the town; the fact that the latter were no palatial 'homes from home' was scarcely the fault of those who, within their often dingy walls, dutifully poured tea, day in day out. There was the Salvation Army's Red Shield in Castle Street and also at Harlescott; YMCAs in Claremont Hill and at Ditherington, canteens at the railway station and at Wyle Cop Schools, a Catholic Women's League at 6a High Street, and perhaps best known of all, 'The Happy Thought' in Chester Street. From 20th December 1939 until the end of the war the Chester Street canteen, which also provided over-night accommodation, never once closed its doors. A proud record. But where did the serviceman with a civilian girlfriend take her for a coffee in an evening? Alas, there was nowhere.

The chaplain at the Barracks appealed in November 1940 on behalf of his flock for citizens to invite soldiers into their homes. "Thereby some have entertained angels unawares" he quoted, adding "I cannot guarantee the angels but I can guarantee real gratitude". In other ways too did people perform small acts of service. When the Priory Boys staged a play, 'Tons of Money', in April 1940 they put on an extra performance for the troops. Three soldiers and eight ATS turned up! More significantly, there was the scheme whereby car owners drove service personnel from the station home on leave. Gifts of money, cigarettes, books and knitted garments were common. It was also not unknown for absent soldiers, sailors and airmen to have their gardens and allotments tended by kindly neighbours.

Of course the troops' credit did not stand universally and perpetually high. Its balance fluctuated but tended to depreciate as the war grew older. There were controversies which flowed and ebbed. One such, early in the war, concerned the fact that local government employees in the forces were having their pay made up. Oddly, this worried the civilian population more than it did those troops who were not so privileged. In June 1940 it was noticed, not entirely with approbation, that British Expeditionary Force men home from Dunkirk were inclined to an excess of high spirits, and as a corollary one may note that in World War Two civilian resentment of young men not in uniform was much less strong than in the first war. The whole white feather syndrome was in any case weakened by the tendency (in contrast to 1914–18) for servicemen to wear 'civvies' while on leave: the potential victim was less easily identifiable.

While little was said against Wrens and WAAFs, the ATS girls, many of whom worked at the Pay Corps office in the Music Hall, seem to have attracted some hostility. They were popularly supposed to enjoy privileges in pay and concessions denied to the majority. They were criticised for eating elevenses in the Square, even for unnecessarily wearing uniform – because they considered it glamorous. This last was too much for one sceptic. "Ye Gods" he wrote "have you seen some of them? Seen their expensive, well-fitting tunics? Their shirts with the sleeves (if the collar fits) buttoning under the armpits, or vice versa if they button at the wrists, the collar showing as much as one expects to see of Mae West? There was one girl who was so upright that I asked her whether she had been drilled by the Guards. I was most embarrassed when she told me she found it a bit awkward to bend as the tail of the shirt would insist upon coming out of the skirt band".

"Shrewsbury?" one ATS exclaimed, "the blessed place gives me a pain in the neck". What many service personnel resented was the trivial nature of the complaints they were so used to hearing. An Air Force sergeant quoted some examples: "... missed my bus again ... five hours queue for panto ... who's pinched my railings?", while another serviceman wrote "Would that some magic carpet could transport Shrewsbury to some front-line area where its people could learn tolerance". But in fairness, with the war by now far advanced, nerves on all sides were becoming frayed – which gave an extra-sharp cutting edge to that stock remark whenever an old acquaintance, on leave, was encountered in the street: "You here again?" and, after a decent pause, "When are you going back?".

Discussion about post-war planning really dated from March 1943 and a speech Churchill made on the subject, and gradually the idea began to dawn that there really was going to be an afterwards to plan for. The leader writer of the Shrewsbury Chronicle commented thus: "Shrewsbury is one of the lucky towns which has derived commercial benefit from the war". Property prices were high, there was a keen demand for unrationed goods, places of entertainment were full. But who was going to pay for post-war development? Would resources be concentrated in the big cities? How would Shrewsbury cope with the employment problem? Would the borough expand or contract? For what population should they plan?

Whatever the authorities might or might not be doing, public interest ran high, and one question that much occupied them was how to commemorate the fallen, once the war was over? Not by another monument – that much was certain. No one wanted another Archangel Michael, in the Quarry or elsewhere. Instead there were many, and more practical, suggestions: a sports complex in Castle Meadows, a public hall in the Square, a new Salop Infirmary on Priory Ridge or near the Column or even at Sundorne Castle. Some wanted a new housing estate (a colony of homes, it was called then) for ex-servicemen, others an old people's home. Why not give Ditherington a clean-up? Extend the Quarry across the river into Becks Field? Acquire and preserve a tract of countryside? Undoubtedly there was more talk then than there was action later.

Meanwhile certain planning decisions were being taken by the council. Both the Smithfield and the Shirehall were to move. Houses would be built at Crowmoor Lane. A road development scheme was approved involving a widened Smithfield Road, a new Welsh Bridge and a loop road crossing Frankwell Quay by viaduct – an imaginative plan which prompted the Chronicle to observe "Mr. Ward (the Borough Surveyor) is planning not for a generation but for a century". Also envisaged were what is now Telford Way and, as has been mentioned, a north-south by-pass.

Nevertheless, policy for the future lagged behind – well behind – the dreams and speculations of private individuals and organisations. Rotary expressed doubts about Harlescott as a site for the new cattle market; they thought Sutton Lane or Wood Street more suitable. The Young Liberals conjured up a vision of the Ditherington Canal as an open-air lido, and why not a riverside park at Preston Boats? Indeed, riverside development was a constant theme, with promenades suggested and a boulevard along Smithfield Road. Some ideas were practical and mundane – to do with industrial growth for example; others more romantic and more fanciful. From the slopes of Claremont Bank would arise a Floral Hall, a Memorial Theatre and a Pump Room with resident orchestra, but not only has it not happened yet, it seems doubtful if it ever will.

In council the controversy centred on what they could afford and what they could not afford to do without. Fancy schemes were all very well but as the Chronicle put it they would "have to go slow with the building of all our fairy castles". Fairy castles maybe, but what about houses?

Two questions dominated people's minds where council housing was concerned. Where would the houses be built and who would be allocated them? In the event the main concentration was to be to the north and east, an arrangement that not everyone agreed with. Said one dissentient "The west side of town will be the preserve of that section of the community who can best afford remoteness from the scene of employment", while another disapproved of putting "the working people around Harlescott and the middle-class around Port Hill".

In the Shrewsbury Chronicle, the borough's housing committee found one of its fiercest critics. A leading article stated "The local authorities are supposed to be making preparations but they are not in any hurry because all the members and all the officials are already well housed", and went on to suggest that wives of servicemen should be co-opted on the committee. There was small likelihood of that if the treatment already meted out to certain of those wives was any guide. In January 1945 the wife of a soldier serving in Italy asked for her name to be put down for one of the Portal houses which were going up, only to be told to come back when they were built. The same month another lady who applied for a house was asked "What if your husband does not return?" Little wonder if the impression gained was one of slight concern on the part of officialdom for the families of those most directly concerned with winning the war.

Local government was beset by a further controversy from 1944 onwards. It started with the announcement in January that the Education department would be taking on five new permanent officials to help administer the new Act, and it continued for another eighteen months as top council posts fell vacant and were filled by men who if they drank tea had not drunk it in the mess or in the NAAFI. "We do not think" said the council, referring to those education appointments, "that likely applicants for these positions are in the services". Once again the Chronicle protested. As similar appointments continued to be made (Clerk to the Council, Town Clerk, Borough Surveyor, Water Engineer) so the criticism mounted: "The chief administrative posts in Shrewsbury will be filled for the next generation by men who have ... obtained exemption from service". "All the best jobs are going to men who have escaped military service but we can find no one to support our protests. Even the British Legion remains silent. We wonder why?". In fact support was forthcoming, but from individuals, for example the gentleman who affirmed on 26th May 1944 that the council should consider those at present fighting rather than "those who happen to be members of any particular craft which still seems to control much or all council matters in Shrewsbury". And this on 11th August: "It seems to me that there will be not much left to us by the time the reserved occupations have had their pick. I trust that the supply of matches and boot laces is not threatened". The theme was later taken up by a soldier's wife: "What are they going to get when they return? Not even a square deal but only just what the men left at home have chosen to leave them, and believe me that will be little". The bitterness was not alleviated by the knowledge that certain other local authorities had had the grace to appoint on a temporary basis only.

In these and other ways were relationships between servicemen and civilians impaired as the war neared its close. Although the demob. system based on age and length of service had been generally approved throughout the forces, dissatisfaction was felt over the lack of urgency with which it seemed to operate, and over such matters as gratuities and war pensions. Nor had troops still overseas been overjoyed to read of VE celebrations at home while they themselves continued to risk their lives. Men returning to Britain were welcomed of course, and those who had been prisoners-of-war were feted. Nevertheless the feeling was that those who had spent the war at home and those who had served – particularly who had served overseas – would take a little while to become used to one another.